Understanding Social Media

UNDERSTANDING
MEDIA
ECOLOGY

Lance Strate
General Editor

Vol. 12

The Understanding Media Ecology series is part
of the Peter Lang Media and Communication list.
Every volume is peer reviewed and meets
the highest quality standards for content and production.

PETER LANG
New York • Bern • Berlin
Brussels • Vienna • Oxford • Warsaw

Robert K. Logan and Mira Rawady

Understanding Social Media

Extensions of Their Users

PETER LANG

New York • Bern • Berlin

Brussels • Vienna • Oxford • Warsaw

Library of Congress Cataloging-in-Publication Data

Names: Logan, Robert K. | Rawady, Mira.
Title: Understanding social media: extensions of their users / Robert K. Logan and
Mira Rawady.
Description: New York: Peter Lang, 2021.
Series: Understanding media ecology; vol. 12
ISSN 2374-7676 (print) | ISSN 2374-7684 (online)
Includes bibliographical references.
Identifiers: LCCN 2021009363 (print) | LCCN 2021009364 (ebook)
ISBN 978-1-4331-8674-5 (hardback) | ISBN 978-1-4331-8675-2 (paperback)
ISBN 978-1-4331-8676-9 (ebook pdf)
ISBN 978-1-4331-8677-6 (epub) | ISBN 978-1-4331-8678-3 (mobi)
Subjects: LCSH: Social media. | Internet—Social aspects.
Classification: LCC HM742 .L64 2021 (print) | LCC HM742 (ebook) |
DDC 302.23/1—dc23
LC record available at https://lccn.loc.gov/2021009363
LC ebook record available at https://lccn.loc.gov/2021009364
DOI 10.3726/b18273

Bibliographic information published by **Die Deutsche Nationalbibliothek.**
Die Deutsche Nationalbibliothek lists this publication in the "Deutsche
Nationalbibliografie"; detailed bibliographic data are available
on the Internet at http://dnb.d-nb.de/.

© 2021 Peter Lang Publishing, Inc., New York
80 Broad Street, 5th floor, New York, NY 10004
www.peterlang.com

This book is dedicated to our families: The Logan and Rawady families

Table of Contents

Preface: What Is/Are Social Media?—The Scope of *Understanding Social Media*

The Purpose of This Book

The purpose of this book is to understand the nature of social media and the impact they are having on almost all aspects of modern-day existence from family life and social interactions to education and commerce. Just as fish are unaware of the water they swim in and we humans are unaware of the air that we breathe so it is that the users of social media are unaware of the effects of these media and take their existence as a natural part of their environment. It is our intention to reveal the effects of social media on their users, how they are changing the nature of our social interactions and how we through our interaction with social media have become actual extensions of our social media, the reverse of McLuhan's notion that media are extensions of mankind.

Who is this Book Intended For?

For the generations of today's parents and grandparents this book will be a guide to the media that are changing the way our kids are growing up so differently from what we experienced when we were kids. Of course, every generation is confronted with a new set of circumstances but the changes for the last two generations with digital media, especially the last one with social media, has never been greater. For young folks this book will also be important as it will provide them with a guide to how social media are controlling their lives contrary to their belief that they are in control of how they use social media. A lesson from Marshall McLuhan and his famous one-liner, 'the medium is the message', is that the greatest impact from a medium is not its content but the way it changes the way we live and the impacts it has on all aspects of our lives. Another lesson from McLuhan is that the effects of media are subliminal because we focus on their content rather than how they create a new environment in which we operate. We hope our study will allow the users of social media to see the impacts of their involvement with social media of which they are unaware.

What is the Scope of Our Study: What Exactly Are Social Media?

When we were beginning our study of social media we debated whether VoIP (Voice over Internet Protocol) apps like Zoom or Skype should be classified as social media. VoIP is nothing more than multi-media telephony using IP instead of the public switching telephone network. Therefore, it follows that if VoIP is social media or a social medium then the telephone is a social medium and hence a form of social media. This raises all kinds of interesting questions. What is (or are) social media anyway? If talking on the telephone is social media then isn't talking face to face also a form of social media. Isn't that also the case for any of the following forms of social media by that definition: the family, schools, clans, tribes, cities, nations, social societies, clubs, churches, temples, synagogues, mosques, armed forces, businesses, governments, organizations, friendships, dating, postal system correspondences, publications of all kinds, radio and TV shows, games, sports, card games, gambling and society in general. In short any and all interactions of humans are transmitted through some form of social media.

Then we thought what about the interactions of animals that interact in families, herds, flocks, schools (of fish), colonies (of insects) and even the interactions of plants, fungi and bacteria because all living organisms communicate with each other and hence their interactions are social. Where do we draw the line? What is the definition of social media, anyway? Well, first we drew the line with humans and do not consider the social media of non-human organisms, although the idea of considering the social media of non-human living organisms would an interesting topic for biologists. Are the colorful plumages of birds a display serving the same purpose as Facebook or maybe Tinder as the peacock's tail feathers facilitates hookups? Are animal cries like email or perhaps Zoom not VoIP but VoSW (voice over sound waves)? Birds definitely tweet. All interesting questions, but we will confine ourselves to human social media.

Next, we could have included in our study of social media all of the human forms of social media that do not involve computers and the Internet as we listed above. Once again, we had to draw the line to exclude the non-digital media and forms of social interaction which are interesting topics, but best addressed by sociologists. We therefore confine ourselves to an analysis of digital-based social media and make use of a media ecology perspective to understand how they have changed the nature of human interactions both digitally and non-digitally especially our face-to-face interactions.

Another issue we need to consider is whether the term 'social media' is singular or plural. Is Facebook a social medium or social media? The same goes for all the social media that we will discuss such as Tinder, email, VoIP, Instagram, Snapchat, Reddit, blogs, Twitter, and YouTube. As to whether or not the term 'social media' is singular or plural we have taken the position that it just depends on the context. In the title of our book Understanding Social Media the term is definitely plural as is the case with the first definition of social media below. In the next three definitions, however, it is singular since the definitions contain the expression 'social media' is denoting social media is singular. All four definitions make it clear, however, that the term 'social media' is confined to those media that are Internet and computer based.

Definition of social media: forms of electronic communication (such as websites for *social* networking and microblogging) through which users create online communities to share information, ideas, personal messages, and other content [such as videos]

(https://www.merriam-webster.com/dictionary/social%20media accessed March 3, 2019).

Social media is the collective of online communications channels dedicated to community-based input, interaction, content-sharing and collaboration. Websites and applications dedicated to forums, microblogging, social networking, social book marking, social curation and wikis are among the different types of social media (https://whatis.techtarget.com/definition/social-media accessed March 3, 2019).

Social media is computer-based technology that facilitates the sharing of ideas, thoughts, and information through the building of virtual networks and communities. By design, social media is internet-based and gives users quick electronic communication of content. Content includes personal information, documents, videos, and photos. Users engage with social media via computer, tablet or smartphone via web-based software or web application, often utilizing it for messaging (https://www.investopedia.com/terms/s/social-media.asp accessed March 3, 2019).

> Social media is defined as "a group of Internet-based applications that build on the ideological and technological foundations of Web 2.0 and that allow the creation and exchange of User Generated Content."
>
> (https://en.wikipedia.org/wiki/Social_media_as_a_public_utility accessed March 3, 2019)

What is Our Methodology and the Historic Background of this Study?: McLuhan's Approach to Media Studies

Given that we will be using a McLuhanesque/media ecology perspective to study social media and their impacts we thought it wise to provide a summary of McLuhan's approach to the study of media and their effects for those not familiar with his work. For a more complete discussion of McLuhan's approach to understanding media the reader is referred to the following books of Marshall McLuhan: *The Gutenberg Galaxy* (McLuhan 1962) and Understanding Media (McLuhan 1964). Additional insights into McLuhan's approach to the study of media and the application of McLuhan's methodology to the digital media he never encountered can be found in the following books of Bob Logan: *McLuhan Misunderstood* (Logan 2013); *Understanding New Media* (Logan 2013); and *McLuhan in Reverse* (Logan in press).

For the convenience of the readers not that familiar with McLuhan's here is a summary of his approach to media ecology that comes from Chapter Two of Logan's recent book *McLuhan in Reverse* (ibid.) Logan describes the 10 elements of McLuhan's approach to studying media as follows:

1. Probes: McLuhan made use of probes to explore the effects of media. He was more interested in making discoveries than in always being correct. Some of his probes did not pan out exactly as planned but on the whole the many predictions he made for the effects of electric media turned out to describe the media of the digital age which he never had a chance to experience as he died in 1980 long before the Internet, the Web and smartphones had arrived.

2. Figure/ground: the key element in McLuhan's general theory of media. Figure/ground analysis is based on the idea that one cannot understand an object of study in isolation from the system or environment in which it operates. Almost all media analysis that were made before McLuhan focused on the content of media rather than the effects of the media independent of their content. McLuhan reversed the focus from studying the content of media to studying the effects of the media independent of their content. This led to his famous aphorism "the medium is the message."

3. The medium is the message: this one-liner is the key element in McLuhan's understanding of media. It incorporates this reversal of attention from figure to ground. The content is the figure and the medium is the ground or environment. "The medium is the message" incorporates the notion that one needs to focus on the effects of a medium independent of its content to understand what its message is.

4. The subliminal nature of ground or environment revealed only by the creation of an anti-environment. Because most people focus on the content of a medium and not its effects independent of its content the ground in which a medium operates is subliminal. It therefore takes an artist or a scientist to be able to create what McLuhan calls an anti-environment to be able to see the subliminal effects of the ground in which a medium operates.

5. The reversal of cause and effect among other reversals: McLuhan's approach to understanding the effects of media involves a number of reversals such as his focus on ground rather than figure. Another reversal is his focus on effects rather than causes and their reversal such as his observation that the effect of the telegraph was the cause of the telephone. Other reversals include his focus on the medium rather than its content; on percepts rather than concepts [see (6)]; and his notion that when a medium is pushed far enough it flips into its opposite which we will discuss below in (10) when we describe his Laws of Media.

6. The importance of percept over concept, the human sensorium and media as extensions of man: Just as McLuhan made a distinction between figure and ground as well as cause and effect and reversed the emphasis of these pairs beginning with the latter and then finally getting around to the former, he made a similar reversal with concepts and percepts. Percepts are ground and concepts are the figure. He was focused on the effects of a medium or technology on the sensorium, i.e. how it affected our senses.

7. The division of communication into the oral, written, and electric ages and the notions of acoustic and visual space: McLuhan treated all forms

of technology whether they involved communication or not as media. However, communication media in terms of the spoken word, written communication and electrically configured information played a particularly important role in McLuhan's analysis of media and technology. Oral and electric communication basically operate in acoustic space and written communication operates in visual space. Oral is acoustic and writing is visual but electric is again acoustic for McLuhan because information comes to from all directions at once as is the case with electric information. With writing one can only see one line of text at a time and one word at a time and hence visual space is linear and sequential. With acoustic information and speech information could come at one simultaneously and from all directions, McLuhan therefore defined acoustic space as having its center everywhere and its margins nowhere.

8. McLuhan's notion of the Global Village is contained in the following quote: "Today, after more than a century of electric technology, we have extended our central nervous system itself in a global embrace, abolishing both space and time as far as our planet is concerned (McLuhan 1964, 3)." McLuhan's notion of the Global Village became a reality after his passing with the emergence of the Net and the Web.

9. Media as environments and media ecology: McLuhan regarded media as environments as the following quotes indicate: "Any understanding of social and cultural change is impossible without a knowledge of the way media work as environments (McLuhan and Fiore 1967, 26)." McLuhan's notion of media as environments led to the notion of media ecology that some claim was first coined by Neil Postman and still others by Eric McLuhan. What is important, however, is that it was McLuhan's notion of media as environments that led to the notion of media ecology.

10. The Laws of Media: towards the end of his career McLuhan formulated his Laws of Media consisting of the following four laws (McLuhan, M. & E. 1988):

Every medium, technology or human-made artifact

1. Enhances some human function.
2. In doing so, it obsolesces some former medium, technology, or human-made artifact, which was used to achieve the same function earlier.
3. In achieving its function, the new medium, technology or human-made artifact retrieves some older form from the past that has been obsolesced.

4. And when pushed far enough, the new medium, technology or human-made artifact reverses or flips into a complementary or possibly an opposite form.

These laws are not exact laws like the laws of physics but they are probes that help explain the evolution of media and technologies. To illustrate how the Laws of Media work we have applied them social media.

Social Media

Enhance one's self image and promote one's self to others;
Obsolesce: the intimacy of face-to-face interactions;
Retrieve: stereotypic social identities or roles from the past;
Reverse or flip into: fake identities and the lack of intimacy.

As we treat each individual social media app and platform we will begin our discussion with a Laws of Media (LOM) or tetrad analysis in which we describe what each app or platform enhances, obsolesces, retrieves and finally reverses or flips into.

The Historic Background of This Study

Given that our analysis will be based on the media ecology approach developed by Marshall McLuhan (1962, 1964, and 1967), and by Robert Logan (2004a) this book may be regarded, in a certain sense, as part of a series of three books initiated by Marshall McLuhan with his amazing 1964 book, *Understanding Media: Extensions of Man*. The second book in this series is the 2004 book by Robert K. Logan (2004a) *Understanding New Media: Extending Marshall McLuhan*. This book *Understanding Social Media: Extensions of Its Users* is intended as the third book in the understanding media series. We hope the reader will not consider us presumptuous. We are not suggesting that our books, the second and the third in the series, are comparable to McLuhan's classic *Understanding Media*. They are not; but our two books have been inspired by *Understanding Media: Extensions of Man* and they are an attempt to carry on the media ecology tradition that McLuhan initiated. In the second book, *Understanding New Media*, the topic of social media was treated, but only in a single chapter. In the 16 years since the publication of that book, social media have grown in importance and have tended to dominate the lives of the users of the Internet and smartphones especially among millennials and those even younger such as Gen Z. This is why we undertook this book-length treatment of social media.

Every technology as Marshall McLuhan observed creates both service and disservice. The services of technologies are obvious as they are the motivation that inspired their invention and they are the reasons for using them. The disservices of technology are subliminal, are independent of their content and are for the most part ignored. We plan to reveal these subliminal aspects of the use of social media by making use of a media ecology perspective based on the ideas developed by McLuhan.

Our study will also be enriched by combining our different experiences and perspectives with social media. One of us (RKL), the old timer, grew up before television and, of course, computers, the Internet and smartphones but has analyzed the full gamut of media and had the good fortune to collaborate with Marshall McLuhan. The other co-author (MR) is a millennial who has just completed her bachelor studies and who, unlike her co-author, is an expert user of a smart phone and many of the online social media apps. Mira is immersed in the new media environment but because of her academic training is able to look at them objectively. She strives to control them and not have them control her. With a gap of two generations (Bob born in 1939 and Mira in 1997) the reader will benefit from the perspective of an active social media user, Mira, and a person, Bob, who lived most of his life without social media and whose social media experience now is basically limited to LinkedIn, email and Zoom, the occasional use of Twitter and as a visitor to YouTube and the Facebook pages of friends. He also does not own a smartphone as for his purposes his MacBook and his home phone serve all his information and social needs. We hope to provide insights into the impacts of the digital, online and smart phone media that are so dramatically changing our world.

A Summary of What the Reader Can Expect

Because social media are built on the platforms of the Internet, the World Wide Web and the smartphone which are themselves based on computing, writing, and the spoken word, we shall begin our analysis of social media in Chapter One of Part I by first considering the seven modes and hence the seven ages of communication to provide the context for the emergence of social media. The seven ages in the order in which they emerged are: (1) pre-verbal mimesis; (2) the spoken word; (3) the written word via ideograms, the alphabet and then typographic print; (4) electric mass media; (5) computers; (6) networking via the Internet and LANs; and (7) the ubiquitous smart phone.

We continue in Part I by describing in greater detail the impacts of the four elements that were essential for the emergence of social media, namely computers in Chapter Two, the Internet and World Wide Web in Chapter Three, smartphones in Chapter Four and online communication channels such as email, IM, texting, VoIP and online meeting apps in Chapter Five.

In Part II we describe the various social media apps and their impacts starting in Chapter Six with the general impact of social media as a class of apps. We then describe the dominant social media including Facebook (Chapter Seven); Instagram (Chapter Eight); Snapchat (Chapter Nine); Reddit (Chapter Ten); Tinder (Chapter Eleven); Blogs (Chapter Twelve); YouTube (Chapter Thirteen), TikTok (Chapter Fourteen) and Twitter (Chapter Fifteen). We have focused on what we consider to be the dominant social media players in this ever-expanding area of online life, which according to Wikipedia (https://en.wikipedia.org/wiki/List_of_social_networking_websites accessed on April 1, 2020) consists of over 180 sites that we have listed in the Appendix.

In Part III we examine the emergence of monopolies in the pre-digital age (Chapter Sixteen); their emergence in the digital age and why they have become so dominant (Chapter Seventeen); the nature of the social media monopolies (Chapter Eighteen); and the role of branding and advertising in social media (Chapter Nineteen).

In Part IV, we conclude our study by examining how the Internet has fractured into the Splinternet as non-democratic regimes try to control the Internet fare in their respective countries (Chapter Twenty). We then examine cyberwarfare and the role that social media plays in it (Chapter Twenty-One). In Chapter Twenty-Two, the final chapter of the book, we turn to the social media counter revolution, the movement within the social media community that believes the excessive use of social media have had a number of negative consequences and that steps need to be taken to limit the misuses of social media.

In the Appendix we provide: (i) a list of social media sites, (ii) a timeline for the launch of these social media sites and (iii) their Alexa Internet page rankings.

Bibliographic Background of the Study of Social Media

There have been many analyses of social media from various perspectives such as attention economy, Marxism, feminism, and surveillance capitalism to mention a few. Among these we call attention to *Surveillance Capitalism* (Zuboff 2019), *The Platform Society* by (Van Dijck, Poell & De Waal) *The Costs of Connection*

(Couldry & Mejias 2019). The reader can find hundreds of analyses online at a site entitled Bibliography of Research on Social Network Sites (http://www.danah. org/researchBibs/sns.php, accessed Jan. 13, 2021). The focus of our study, however, as we described above, is to analyze social media from the perspective of Marshall McLuhan's analysis and understanding of media and their effects. The studies that have been made to date from a McLuhan/media ecology perspective include Paul Levinson's (2016) *McLuhan* in an Age of *Social Media*; a collection of essays in the book *McLuhan: Social Media Between Faith and Culture* edited by Logan and Pietropaolo (2015); Chapter 43 in my book *Understanding New Media*: Extending Marshall McLuhan (Logan 2016); Thomas Cooper's (2020) article "*McLuhan, Social Media* and Ethics;" and Geoffrey Johnston's 2015 article entitled "Marshall McLuhan's Ideas Applied to Social Media"

(https://mcluhangalaxy.wordpress.com/2015/11/14/marshall-mcluhans-ideas-applied-to-social-media/, accessed Jan. 13, 2021).

Reader Feedback

We have written this book in the spirit of Marshall McLuhan as a probe and an exploration. We therefore welcome comments from our readers as to whether or not our probe has revealed for you any new aspect of McLuhan's work or your understanding of social media that you did not entertain before reading this book. We regard a scholarly book as a dialogue between the author and their readers. We therefore ask you to kindly sent us your comments by email to logan@physics.toronto.ca and I look forward to your communication and I will reply to all of your email posts.

Acknowledgements

Many of the ideas in this book are those of Marshall McLuhan and those that are ours were informed by him and other media ecologists we have referenced. We also wish to acknowledge the contributions of members of the media ecology community and in particular those of Corey Anton, Eva Berger, Adriana Braga, Roman Kordiuk, Alex Kuskis, Andrey Miroshnichenko, Izabella Pruska-Oldenhof, Anat Ringel and Ed Tywoniak. In addition, Bob Logan wishes to acknowledge the contributions of his students at St. Michael's College, University of Toronto who took his two seminar courses McLuhan and What is Information? with particular mention of Emily Findlay White, Marlie Tandoc, Zeynep Merve Iseri and Kateryna Gromova. We also wish to acknowledge and thank St. Michael's College, University of Toronto for creating the stimulating environment in which we carried out the research for this book.

PART I

THE MEDIA THAT MADE
SOCIAL MEDIA POSSIBLE

CHAPTER ONE

Introducing the Seven Ages of Communication

In the past 80 years in rapid succession we have experienced three communication revolutions:

1. the emergence of digital computing, i.e. mainframe computers;
2. personal computers;
3. online communication with the Internet and the World Wide Web; and
4. the smart phone.

Never before in the history of humankind have we experience such a rapid turnover of communication strategies or devices. Speech has been with us 50–100 thousand years and mimesis or non-verbal communication is even older than that. We have made use of written texts for the past 5,000 years and electric media for the past 200 years. However, in the past 80 years we have had the emergence of four new modes of communication, i. digital mainframe computers, ii. personal computers, iii. online media with the Internet and the World Wide Web and iv. the smart phone.

Each one of these new media forms have had a major impact on our educational, social, commercial and political systems. Each changed the way we communicate, the way we think, the way we see the world, the way we interact with each other physically, emotionally, commercially, and socially. It changed the way we organize our activities, our work, our play, our families, our governments, and our educational systems. Each new form of communication ushers in a new way in which we organize our lives. The figure of each of the categories we just listed will change as the ground in which they operate changes and that ground has changed with the emergence of social media as it did with the emergence of computers, the Internet and the Web before them.

Seven Modes of Communication

How do we communicate? Let us count the ways. We communicate:

1. **mimetic**ally with facial gesture, hand signals, body language and non-verbal vocalizations (at least two million years ago); also, aesthetically through the visual arts, music and dance. Here we include all of genus homo, but the remaining modes of communication beginning with speech are uniquely those of our species, Homo sapiens or modern humans.
2. **oral**ly with the spoken word (50–100 thousand years ago);
3. literately with the **written** word, by ideograms such as logograms, hieroglyphics, Chinese characters (starting in 3000 BCE), phonetic alphabets (starting in 1500 BCE) and finally by typographic print (starting in 1436);
4. **electrical**ly by telegraph (1835); telephone (1876); radio (1896); recorded sound: vinyl records (1877)/tape (1930) /CD (1982) players and television (1928);
5. **digital**ly with computers (1941)
6. **online** with local area networks (LAN), the Internet (1969), the World Wide Web (1994) and,
7. **online and mobile** with smart phones (2001) all day long, day in and day out.

(The dates in parentheses are approximate start dates for these different modes of communication and access to information.)

Seven Ages of Communication

Each new way we communicate, each new language dramatically changed the way we, humans, think, the way we see the world, the way we interact with each other physically, emotionally, commercially, and socially. It changed the way we organize our activities, our work, our commerce, our education, our play, our families, our governments and our politics. Each new form of communication ushered in a new age of communication. The seven modes of communication listed above gave rise respectively to

1. The Mimetic Tradition,
2. The Oral Tradition,
3. The Literate Age,
4. The Electric Age,
5. The Digital Age,
6. The Online or Internet/World Wide Web Age,
7. The Age of the Ubiquitous Smart Phone.

Harold Innis (1950, 1972) and Marshall McLuhan (1962, 1964) identified three communication eras or ages, oral, written and electric in their development of the field of media ecology, the field in which they claimed that the media of communication have an impact greater than the content of what they transmit. McLuhan summarized this claim with the one-liner, "the medium is the message." McLuhan further sub-divided the era of written communication into pre-alphabetic literacy, alphabetic-based literacy and typographic print.

Logan (2002), in an article entitled The Five Ages of Communication, claimed that there were two other communication eras in addition to the ones identified by McLuhan. One, which predated verbal spoken language, namely, the mimetic communication of hand signals, facial gestures, body language and non-verbal vocalizations such as grunts, cries, laughs, screams and moans. The other was electronic/digital communication with computers and the Internet, which Logan (2002) distinguished from electric communication that makes use of telegraph, telephone, radio, recording devices and television. In 2002 only eight years after the introduction of the Internet to the public and four years before the introduction of the Blackberry, the first device to marry the smart phone with the Internet, Logan (2002) lumped the Internet and online life together with computers and defined this era as the Digital Age. As it turns out this update of McLuhan three Ages has to be once again revised because of the revolutionary impact of the Net, the Web and the smart phone.

In 2002 the Blackberry, the world's first smartphone was released and by 2012 it had 80 million users but that number has since declined to 11 million today (en.wikipedia.org/wiki/BlackBerry, accessed Feb 27, 2018). The Blackberry, however, paved the way for Apple's iPhone, which has an estimated 700 million users (fortune.com/2017/03/06/apple-iphone-use-worldwide/ accessed, Feb 27, 2018) and the equally ubiquitous Android devices. There are now about 3.5 billion smart-phone users worldwide, a number that continues to climb (www.statista.com/statistics/330695/number-of-smartphone-users-worldwide/, accessed January 27, 2021).

Given the ubiquity of the smart phone and the phenomenal growth of the Internet we have re-evaluated Logan's (2002) claim for five communication ages and now suggest that there are seven communication ages. The justification for the two additional ages is as follows. Given the exponential growth of the Internet and the Web we have divided the digital age into two ages, one dominated by computers before the advent of the Internet, which retains the name of the Digital Age and the other age, dominated by the Internet and the Web that we label as the Online or Internet Age. The smartphone which allows access to the Internet and hence the Online Age 24 × 7 and is continuously growing in the number of users has created a new age which we call the Age of the Ubiquitous Smart Phone or simply the Smart Phone Age.

The justification for the 6th Age, the Online Age is due to the many disruptions of pre-Internet life that the Internet has created among which are the emergence of the following phenomena in the market place and elsewhere in the life of Homo Internetus:

- retail sales (Amazon, eBay; Wayfair);
- grocery sales (Amazon vs supermarkets; will supermarkets become mega convenience stores?);
- travel booking (Expedia); taxicab hailing (Uber uber alles)
- advertising (Google + Facebook);
- socializing (Facebook); and dating (Tinder);
- research (Google);
- distribution of entertainment, video, cinema, music (streaming; YouTube; Netflix; online TV);
- news (decline of newspapers); magazines (Zines);
- warfare; spying; fake news or lying; propaganda, hacking; i.e. cyber warfare
- pornography and sexting;
- fraud (online scams);
- telephone voice overtaken by texting;
- email disrupted telegraphy and caused the demise of Western Union
- retail banking; credit ratings;
- education (online courses; MOOCs; Coursera; continuing education; university credit course; MA & PhD; corporate training);
- knowledge management;
- fundraising (Kickstarter).

The justification for the 7th Age is that the users of smart phones live a significant part of their life online never parting from their online device during their waking hours with many of them having their smart phone at their bed side even when they are asleep. Among the disruptions to pre-smart phone life are the following:

- the decline of face-to-face social interactions even though smart phones were initially thought to facilitate social interactions;
- the decline of family life where family meals do not seem to interrupt the use of the ubiquitous smart phone;
- a lack of awareness of the smart phone users' physical environment as so many users walk indoors and outdoors with their focus on their screen more or less oblivious to their surroundings.

Many smart phone users pay more attention to their phone than to the folks that are physically around them. The quality of their relationships suffers, because they are more interested in the approvals via likes from strangers they do not know instead of developing a close and meaningful relationships with their friends and folks in their immediate environment. The majority of smart phone users socialize face-to-face with their smart phone beside them and frequently they are interacting with their device while socializing with their friends at the same time. They are multitasking as though socializing and scanning their smart phones are tasks of equal importance as is documented by Mira Rawady. She observed that

"at almost every social event that I have participated in, my friends and other attendees are usually on their phone, documenting the outing for Instagram and Twitter instead of actually being present in the moment. It's almost like we go out to share it on social media rather than go out for the sake of enjoyment and the human connection. Knowing that everyone is more concerned with their phone and social platforms as opposed to their present moment activity undermines face to face interactions and socialization. If it's not on Instagram, did you really go out? Did you really go to that concert, or have that meal, or reunite with that friend? Did you really enjoy it? Or was it for the sake of posting content and getting likes? This made me doubt my own social media uses, as I questioned my purpose for documenting my own life."

Smart phones with all their entertainment apps are great time wasters for students. They discourage reading for entertainment as playing games on their phones does not involve any effort like reading a book. Instead of using dead time to think, reflect or meditate smart phone users fill up time while waiting for a bus or walking along the street or even riding an elevator interacting with their smart phone.

The Content of One Communication Age is the Prior Communication Age

Marshall McLuhan (1970, 168) suggested that the content of any medium is the prior medium when he wrote: "The content or time-clothing of any medium is the preceding medium or culture." The content of speech is mimesis in the sense that speech is always accompanied with tone, gesture, hand signals and body language. The content of writing is speech. The written Torah was a transcription of the oral Torah by Ezra, the Scribe who transcribed the oral Torah when the Israelites were in exile in Babylon. The same is the case with Homer's Iliad and Odyssey which were originally part of the ancient Greek oral tradition. According to Islamic tradition the Quran was revealed to Muhammad orally. The sacred texts of the Hindus and the Buddhists were also originally composed orally and then transcribed. Also, Confucian texts were not written by Confucius but by his students after his death based on his sayings.

The content of electric media is writing in the sense that the scripts for radio and television are written. This was also the case for the telegraph. The content of the telephone, on the other hand, is still part of the oral tradition as are radio and television interviews to a certain extent.

The content of computing for the most part is writing. The content of the Internet/Web is writing and electric media such as radio (podcasts), recordings, and television and cinema through streaming.

The content of the smart phone is the Internet/Web, writing for texting and occasionally the oral tradition when the actual phone facility of the smartphone is used.

Paralleling the content of a medium is some prior medium, we suggest that embedded in each communication age is a previous communication age. The content of the Oral Tradition is the Mimetic Tradition and the content of the Literate Age is the Oral Tradition and the content of the Electric Age is the Literate Age and the content of the Digital Age is the Electric Age and the content of the Online Age is the Digital Age and the content of the Age of the Ubiquitous Smart Phone is the Online or Internet Age. The content of the social media, the subject of our study, are the Internet and the World Wide Web.

References

Innis, Harold. 1951. *The Bias of Communication*. Toronto: University of Toronto Press.
Innis, Harold. 1972. *Empire and Communications*. Toronto: University of Toronto Press. (originally published by Oxford University Press in 1950).

Logan, Robert K. 2002. "The Five Ages of Communication." *Explorations in Media Ecology* 1:13–20.

McLuhan, Marshall. 1962. *The Gutenberg Galaxy: The Making of Typographic Man.* Toronto: University of Toronto Press.

McLuhan, Marshall. 1964. *Understanding Media: Extensions of Man.* New York: McGraw Hill. (The page references in the text are for the McGraw Hill paperback second edition. Readers should be aware that the pagination in other editions is different.)

McLuhan, Marshall. 1970. *Culture is Our Business.* New York: McGraw-Hill.

CHAPTER TWO

The Impacts of Digital Computing

LOM: Computing

Enhances: control and manipulation of information and processes;
Obsolesces: the mechanical;
Retrieves: customization;
Reverses or flips into: information overload and "anarchy via the overlay of bureaucracy (McLuhan & McLuhan 1988, 189)".

Introduction

In this chapter we will survey the impact of digital computing or computers. Before recounting the story of digital computing or computers that emerged in the 1940s, we will first survey the many techniques of non-digital computation that preceded this development after which we will examine the impacts of digital computing or computers including main frame computers (including supercomputers and cloud server computers), mini computers and personal computers ranging from desktop to laptop to notebooks to tablets. Although smart phones are basically computers we will not analyze their impacts until we deal with them in Chapter Four.

Non-Digital Computing

The most ancient form of computing or accounting took place in pre-historic times with the appearance of tallies, which are basically notches carved on an animal bone or an antler. Three examples include the Lebombo bone found in the Lebombo mountains located between South Africa and Swaziland that is estimated to be between 44,200 and 43,000 years old; the Wolf bone which was excavated in Moravia and thought to be 30,000 years old; and the Ishango bone circa 19,000 BC found in the Belgian Congo. Tallies do not indicate what is being enumerated but they indicate early forms of human computation and numerosity. Other forms of tallies making use of pebbles or shells have been observed in a variety of cultures in historic time but naturally archeological records of them do not exist.

The next development in non-digital computing devices dating back to 8000 BC is the appearance in excavations throughout the Near East of accounting tokens made of clay in which the shape of the token indicated the agricultural commodity being accounted for Schmandt-Besserat (1978). The next breakthrough in computing came with the invention of writing and a notation for numerals, dating back to 3200 BC in Sumer in Mesopotamia, which Schmandt-Besserat (1986) showed emerged from pressing the clay tokens into clay tablets as a way of preserving the records of economic transactions. The token impression representing the large and small measure of wheat came to represent the numerals 10 and 1 respectively and allowed the creation of a primitive Roman numeral type of numeric notation.

The use of pebble and accounting tokens it is surmised led to the invention of the abacus in Babylon circa 2500 BC, which in a certain sense was the first mechanical computing device. The abacus was greatly improved by the Chinese with the invention of the suan pan circa 200 AD. This device was able to perform other tasks in addition to mere counting. It could for example be used to do addition, subtraction, multiplication, division, square roots and cube roots with great ease and quite rapidly. The abacus based on the original Babylonian and Chinese versions was used all over world and is still in use to this day. Devices similar to the Old-World abacuses were developed in Mesoamerica and a counting device base on knots on colored strings was developed by the Incas in South America.

The next breakthrough in computation was the invention of zero and the place number notation system known as Arabic numerals which first emerged among Hindu mathematicians as early as 200 BC and was subsequently adopted by Arabic mathematicians and transmitted to Europe through trade between Arab and Italian merchants circa 1200 AD, which is why the term Arabic numerals is used to describe the place number system. It was actually Fibonacci who wrote the book Liber Abaci (Book of the Abacus) in 1202 that introduced zero and the place number system to the Europeans. He learned of the Hindu-Arabic numerals while travelling in the Near East with his father, a merchant who traded with his Arab counterparts.

John Napier discovered logarithms and published his results in 1614 in his book *Mirifici Logarithmorum Canonis Descriptio* (A Description of the Wonderful Law of Logarithms). Logarithms greatly facilitated mathematical calculations. It also led to the invention of the slide rule, a device that allowed the rapid calculation of multiplications and divisions as well as square roots, trigonometry, exponents and logarithms. The slide rule was an essential tool for scientists and engineers before the development of electronic calculators and computers.

The next step in automating mathematical calculations came with mechanical calculators. Blaise Pascal invented the first device of this kind in 1642 in order to help his father with the tedious task of calculating tax accounts. Pascal manufactured a small number of his devices. It wasn't until 1851 that the Thomas arithmometer, a mechanical calculator, was developed that could be used reliably in office environments. By 1887 the comptometer featured a keyboard that facilitated the entry of figures. The mechanical calculator held sway until the development of the electronic calculator in the 1970s.

The slide rule and mechanical calculators are examples of analogue computers. A number of special purpose analogue computers were developed to execute specialized tasks such as process control, protective relays, ship navigation, and fire control on ship board cannons. Two notable analogue computers were the tide predicting device invented by James Thomson in 1872 and the differential analyzer built by Vannevar Bush and Harold Hazen in 1927 at MIT that was used to solve differential equations. Once all-purpose digital computers were developed analogue computers became obsolete.

Digital Computing with the Emergence of Computers

General purpose digital computing devices or computers as they are commonly called differ from analogue computers in that they are programmable. The idea that one could build a programmable computer was first conceived by Charles Babbage, an English mechanical engineer in 1883. He never was able to build his computer, which he called an Analytic Engine. Ada Lovelace, who worked with Babbage, wrote and published a program that could have run on Babbage's Analytic Engine. She is recognized and regarded as the world's first computer programmer.

The principle behind all of today's digital computers was developed by Alan Turing in 1936 in which he described what he called a "Universal Computing machine," which today goes by the name of a "universal Turing machine". His ideas were not put to use until the beginning of World War II when scientists were trying to crack the German secret codes generated by the Enigma encryption machine. The first programmable computer, Collosus. was built at Bletchley Park in England and became operational at the beginning of 1944. The second programmable computer, the Eniac, became operational in 1945 at the University of Pennsylvania. These machines were huge using thousands of vacuum tubes and relays. With the development of transistors in 1947 and their displacement of vacuum tubes in 1955 followed by the development of microchips and integrated circuits, computers, in the late 1950s, became much smaller in size.

The first computers were known as mainframe computers which were followed by mini computers. These computers gave rise to what we will call the first-generation computer revolution. The emergence of personal computers in the form of desktop, laptop, notebook and tablet computers gave rise to what we will call the second-generation computer revolution.

The Impacts of Mainframe Computers and Other Large-Scale Computers such as Supercomputers and Servers

Mainframe computers revolutionized scientific and engineering research as well as commerce, education, government and all activities that require the organization of data and information. The name main frame derives from the fact that the components of the early computers such as the central processing unit and the memory banks were house in large cabinets called main frames. The use of mainframe computers also known as general purpose computers were limited to large organizations because of their cost. They were used for bulk data processing such as inventory control, transaction processing, and resource planning. Mainframes were also used by academic and private sector researchers and by governments for administration. In the commercial world one of the impacts of costly computing was that the efficiencies that were realized by large organizations that could afford these devices favored large commercial enterprises over those of smaller enterprises. A prime example of this is the way that the efficiencies of computing allowed Walmart to offer more competitive prices for the products they sold driving many local merchants out of business. Computers also allowed them to manage a large network of stores with the effect that they could get better pricing from their suppliers through bulk purchasing that smaller retail operations were unable to negotiate. This again allowed them to offer their products at still lower prices than their competitors.

In the 1960s supercomputers came on stream that were capable of much faster processing speeds measured in floating-point operations per second or FLOPS. By 2017 speeds of nearly 10^{17} FLOPS were reached. These machines are used basically for scientific research and largescale engineering processes.

Another class of big computers are servers that allow users at terminals or personal computers linked into the server to make use of applications or data bases resident on the server. Server networks were the forerunners of the Internet as they demonstrated the usefulness of sharing computer-based assets among a network of users. Servers also allow a group of users to make use of a shared facility such as a printer or a fax machine.

Minicomputers and Microcomputers (i.e. Personal Computers)

The minicomputer was a smaller and cheaper version of mainframe computers that had a short life span. They first appeared in the mid 1960s and their demise began in the mid 1980s and the early 1990s when they were replaced by personal computers that were linked by LANs (local area networks).

The microcomputer or the personal computer makes its first appearance in the late 1970s and early 1980s as a desktop computer. It democratized computing and brought computing from the world of work into one's home and ushered in the era of personal computing. It was the beginning of a revolution as big as the computer revolution of the 1940s and was not something that computer experts at IBM in 1968 could imagine as the following story will illustrate:

Marshall McLuhan who never saw a personal computer during his lifetime nevertheless predicted its arrival as his friend and colleague, Arthur Porter, related in the following reminiscence of a 1968 luncheon that McLuhan had with a number of IBM executives:

> Mac Hillock, [an IBMer] arranged a lunch with half a dozen of IBM's divisional directors. Marshall got soon tuned up and was telling them about a computer for every home, no need to visit the grocery store … Two of them said to me after lunch, "we have not heard of anything as crazy as that!" Marshall was talking about the personal computer a dozen years before they thought of it. Here was a professor of English more than a decade ahead of the technical people in computer evolution. He was thinking in terms of the user (Nevitt & McLuhan 1994, 29–30).

The IBM executives were not the only ones who could not imagine that personal computers would come to be a major if not dominant form of computing. Ken Olsen, founder of Digital Equipment Corporation, the leading manufacturer of mini computers opined in 1977: "There is no reason anyone would want a computer in their home." The ironic aspect of this prediction that was so off the mark is that it was made in the same year that Wozniak and Jobs released the Apple II computer that took the world by storm. Another example of a prediction that was made way off the mark was made in 1943 at the very beginning of the computer age by the president of IBM, Thomas Watson who said, "I think there is a world market for maybe five computers."

With the success of personal computers there are a lot more than five computers in the world today. It is estimated that there are upwards of 4 billion Internet users worldwide (https://www.internetworldstats.com/stats.htm, accessed March 22, 2018) and hence an equal number of computers where we have included tablets and smart phones as computers.

The Personal Computer Revolution

The personal computer revolution started with hobbyist building their own computers using readily available electronic components. The most influential of these early pioneers of personal computing was the team of Steve Wozniak, who designed the Apple I computer and his business partner Steve Jobs the marketing genius that made Apple into the most valued company in the world. Apple went on to became the first company in the world to achieve a valuation of one trillion dollars and most recently the first to achieve a valuation of two trillion dollars. The personal computer revolution began in 1976 when Jobs and Wozniak formed a company to manufacture and market the Apple I computer, which they sold for $666.66. Working out of the Jobs family garage, they netted nearly $800,000, which allowed them to capitalize their next venture which was the design and manufacture of the Apple II computer. The Apple II took the computer market by storm netting them $139 million in sales in the first three years of operation. By 1980 the company was worth $1.2 Billion and was being publicly traded. The next step for Apple was the MacIntosh in 1984, the first computer with a graphic user interface (GUI) that took advantage of the design genius of Jobs. After being pushed out of Apple in 1985 by the CEO that Jobs had hired, he returned to Apple in 1997 and instigated a series of product developments that changed the landscape of personal computing with the release of a string of revolutionary products and services including the MacOS and MaciOS operating systems, the iPod, the iTunes store, the iPad and the iPhone. Although these products or services were not the first of their kind they were the most elegantly designed in the market place and dominated each of the markets that they entered. Perhaps the most important aspect of the personal computer revolution was the way in which it democratized computing so that the computer population of the world grew from 5 in 1943 to over a billion 65 years later in 2018.

The Impact of Computing

There is hardly an area of human endeavour that is not impacted by computing ranging from science, engineering, scholarship, communications, the arts, commerce, manufacturing, logistics, education and healthcare. Computers are embedded in our buildings, automobiles, telephones, appliances, and equipment of every kind and variety. Networked computing gave rise to the Internet and eventually the World Wide Web so that it is impossible to discuss the impact of computing without at the same time discussing the Net and the Web. We will therefore wait until the next chapter where we will discuss the impact of the Internet to discuss the joint impact of computing with the Net and the Web. In the mean time we look at the impact of Artificial Intelligence (AI) and robotics whose operation do not depend, for the most part, on the use of the Internet.

Artificial Intelligence (AI) and Robots

Many believe that computers are a form of intelligence because they are able to solve so many problems. The problems that they solve and the questions that they answer, however, are all formulated by the humans that have designed, built and programmed these computers. In our humble opinion, computers no matter how sophisticated they become will never rival human intelligence because they do not and cannot formulate the questions. They lack curiosity, the desire to learn or know more about something because a computer has no desires, purposes, objectives, or goals. A computer cannot have curiosity as curiosity is an emotion and computers are without emotions. Curiosity will have to be programmed into a computer, and hence the curiosity of a computer will be determined by that of its programmers.

There is a danger if we overestimate the potential of AI and believe it can do our thinking for us. There is a notion known as the Technological Singularity that posits that someday through artificial general intelligence an AI computer will program another AI computer and so on by iteration until a singularity is reached such that an AI configured computer will be more intelligent than any human. As just described this is impossible because a computer without emotions, a sense of self and purpose cannot be creative, the most precious characteristic of human intelligence. The danger with the idea of the Singularity is that we will lower our standards as to what constitutes human intelligence to meet the level of intelligence of some AI configured super computer (Braga & Logan 2017).

Without inborn curiosity the intelligence of computers will always be artificial. Nevertheless, AI is a very valuable tool that together with human intelligence has helped solved many important problems and had many benefits for humankind. AI has increased human productivity and efficiency and been a great time saving technology. The application of AI and robotics have reduced the cost of the products and services that we consume. AI has helped scientists to process vast amounts of data they have collected and helped engineers to design better systems. AI has played a crucial role in health care aiding doctors to assess patients and their health risks and prescribe personalized medicine and identify possible side effects of those medicines. AI is the technology behind self-driving cars and other motorized vehicles as well as the automatic piloting of airplanes and ships. AI is being used to search for natural resources in environments that pose dangers to human explorers in places deep underground or at the bottom of the sea. Home automation systems that reduce energy consumption also make use of AI. We encounter AI all the time, for example when we use Google or other search engines, interact with Siri or other automated personal assistants, make use of GPS systems to navigate while driving our cars, and playing video games on our computers or tablets.

References

Braga, Adriana and Robert K. Logan. 2017. "The Emperor of Strong AI Has No Clothes: Limits to Artificial Intelligence." *MDPI Information* 8: 156–77.

McLuhan, Marshall and Eric McLuhan. 1988. *Laws of Media: The New Science*. Toronto: University of Toronto Press.

Nevitt, Barrington and Maurice McLuhan. 1994. *Who Was Marshall McLuhan?* Toronto: Stoddart Books.

Schmandt-Besserat, Denise. 1978. "The earliest precursor of Writing." *Scientific American* 238 (6): 50–58.

Schmandt-Besserat, Denise. 1986. "The Origins of Writing: An Archaeologist's Perspective." *Written Communication* 3 (1): 31–45.

CHAPTER THREE

The Impacts of the Internet and the World Wide Web: The Online Age

Introduction

In this chapter we will describe the Internet (Net) and the World Wide Web (Web) and survey their impact on almost all aspects of human activity. The Internet is a medium whose content is digital computing illustrating Marshall McLuhan's observation that "Except for light, all other media come in pairs, with one acting as the content of the other (McLuhan 1995, 27)." McLuhan (1964, 267) expressed this idea in Understanding Media in the following way:

> Although the medium is the message, the controls go beyond programming. The restraints are always directed to the "content," which is always another medium. The content of the press is literary statement, as the content of the book is speech, and the content of the movie is the novel.

Following McLuhan's lead, we assert that the content of the Internet is digital computing as is the World Wide Web, email, chat rooms, Internet Relay Chat, instant messaging and Usenet newsgroups, as well as the access to other services such as telnet (a network protocol that allows a user on one computer to log into another computer that is part of the same network) and ftp (File Transfer Protocol). The Internet enhances the connectivity of computer users and provides access to information stored on servers now referred to as the Cloud. As a result, it has obsolesced teletype and reduced the usage of fax.

The Internet

LOM: The Internet

Enhances: the connectivity of computer users;
Obsolesces: teletype and fax and the specialist as the source of information;
Retrieves: community as in the global village;
Reverses or flips into: information overload and deception.

The Internet was developed in the United States as a civil defense tool by the American military as an alternative backup communication system in case of a breakdown of the regular communication system due to war especially nuclear war or natural disaster. Its first users were the military and the scientists and engineers who helped create it. The next cohort of users were academics, primarily scientists and engineers once again, who used it to facilitate their research activities, mainly through the use of email and the transfer of data and software files from one computer to another. The Internet proved to be an ideal medium for scientific and other scholarly research because science has always been a collaborative activity in which scientists have shared their data, their ideas and their results freely.

It has since evolved into a universal medium of communication used world-wide. The number of Internet users as of December 2020 is 4.95 billion users or 63.2% of the 7.84 billion people living on the planet (https://www.internetworldstats.com/stats.htm, accessed January 30, 2020). The Internet is the medium that explicitly realized Marshall McLuhan's prediction that electrically configured information would convert the planet into a "global village." The Internet is the public square of that global village.

As described in Wikipedia article (https://en.wikipedia.org/wiki/Internet, accessed March 8, 2020):

> The **Internet** is the global system of interconnected computer networks that use the Internet protocol suite (TCP/IP) to link devices worldwide. It is a *network of networks* that consists of private, public, academic, business, and government networks of local to global scope, linked by a broad array of electronic, wireless, and optical networking technologies. The Internet carries a vast range of information resources and services, such as the inter-linked hypertext documents and applications of the World Wide Web (WWW), electronic mail, telephony and file sharing.

The Internet does not have a central switching system or headquarters or any form of central administration. Rather it is a distributed network making use of telephone and cable company infrastructure, but it is not operated by any telephone company or other form of central administration. The Internet itself is not any particular piece of hardware or software but rather it is the system with a few protocols whereby the activities that take place on this platform are operationalized. The Internet creates its own space, which goes by the name of cyberspace, a term introduced by William Gibson (1984) in his novel *Neuromancer: Cyberspace*. "A consensual hallucination experienced daily by billions of legitimate operators, in every nation, … A graphic representation of data abstracted from the banks of every computer in the human system."

Cyberspace is a virtual space but it is generated by the users of the Internet as their messages are received by a server that disassembles the original message into small data packets that are transmitted and reassembled by the data packet switching protocol known as Internet Protocol (IP) developed by J.C.R. Licklider who proposed the idea at MIT in 1962 and then implemented it at the Advanced Research Projects Agency (ARPA) in what was called the Arpanet, the forerunner of the Internet.

The World Wide Web

LOM: The World Wide Web

Enhances: two-way communication, access to information, and continuous learning;
Obsolesces: print-based academic journals, newspapers, and paper-based communication in general;
Retrieves: alignment and community;
Reverses or flips into: the streaming of the content of mass media including Web games, music, radio, and TV.

There are two developments that made the Internet a popular medium for the general public instead of a specialized tool for scientists and the military application. The first was the large potential user base that the existence of the personal computer made possible as described in Chapter Two. The second was the emergence of the World Wide Web simply known as the Web that allowed the creation of an enormous variety of applications that were of interest to the general public.

Tim Berners-Lee invented the World Wide Web while he was working at CERN, the high energy physics accelerator located in Geneva Switzerland. The problem he wanted to solve was that of the communication among researchers who came to CERN from different parts of the world to conduct experiments there. They needed to share their data and their experimental set ups with each other. He designed the Web using hypertext that allowed the sharing of both visual and textual information. He saw that what he designed would not only be useful to the scientific community at CERN but would also be a useful tool for the general public.

In 1989 Berners-Lee set about designing the Hypertext Transfer Protocol (HTTP) that allowed users to use the Internet to share hypertext designing the world's first Web browser, which he shared with the general public making it available on the Internet. He wrote, "The Web is more a social creation than a technical one. I designed it for a social effect—to help people to work together—and not as a technical toy (Berners-Lee 1999, 123)." After having invented the Web and making it available to the general public Berners-Lee set about to create the World Wide Web Consortium with the mission to create and maintain the standards for the operation of the Web. He also founded the World Wide Web Foundation with the mission to improve the Web and allow it to be used across the globe.

Berners-Lee realized the dream of Vannevar Bush who conceived of an idea similar to hypertext. In the article "As We May Think" that appeared in 1945 issue of the Atlantic Monthly Bush introduced the idea of the Memex (memory and index). It was a hypothetical device that would allow a user to compress and store all of their books, records, and communications. Bush's Memex was not computer based but was conceived as a documented bookmark list of static microfilm pages. The Memex inspired electronic hypertext systems rather than being modeled directly from it.

Inspired by the Memex model, Theodor Nelson (1965) coined the terms "hypertext" and "hypermedia" that have gained common currency in the English language as well as others languages. Hypertext refers to linking different bodies of text using electronic computers in separate documents whereas hypermedia entails linking from one medium to another medium. Wikipedia makes extensive use of hypertext to move the readers from one Wikipedia article to another Wikipedia article or to another Web site. In the case of hypermedia, the linkage would be between two different kinds of media. For example, a hyperlink in a document taking one to an audio or video clip would constitute a hypermedia link. Wikipedia defines hypermedia as

> an extension of the term hypertext, is a nonlinear medium of information which includes graphics, audio, video, plain text and hyperlinks. This contrasts with the broader term multimedia, which may include non-interactive linear presentations as well as hypermedia (en.wikipedia.org/wiki/Hypermedia, accessed March 24, 2020).

Nelson also coined other terms that have not achieved the currency of hypertext and hypermedia. The term *transclusion* is defined as the inclusion of part or all of an electronic document into one or more other documents by hyper-text reference (en.wikipedia.org/wiki/Transclusion). Another term he coined was *intertwingled* and *intertwingularity*. "Everything is deeply intertwingled. In an important sense there are no subjects at all; there is only all knowledge, since the cross-connections among the myriad topics of this world simply cannot be divided up neatly (Nelson 1974)." He added the following comment in the revised edition of his 1974 book: "Hierarchical and sequential structures, especially popular since Gutenberg, are usually forced and artificial. Intertwingularity is not generally acknowledged—people keep pretending they can make things hierarchical, categorizable and sequential when they can't (Nelson 1987, 31)." Nelson claims he first formulated his ideas for hypertext when he was a graduate student at Harvard as early as 1960 when he began what he called Project Xanadu. He later formed a company to commercialize his ideas but Project Xanadu never bore fruit.

The ideas of Bush and Nelson were finally realized by Berners-Lee with the World Wide Web making use of the Internet for the transmission of information. The general public and business community discovered the Internet and its potential for the dissemination of information and ideas with the release of a commercial Web browser by Netscape in 1994. The scientists' ethos of sharing ideas, information and data remained the dominant ethos of the Internet by other communities with a few exceptions of spammers and scammers. For the most part the Internet and the Web retain their unique character as an open medium of communication as it was intentionally designed by Licklider and Berners-Lee.

The use of the Internet is now considered as indispensable for doing business as the telephone, the computer and the fax machine. Many firms such as Ford demand that their suppliers use the Internet to conduct certain aspects of their commercial transactions with them. "Jacque Nasser, [President and CEO of Ford], always reminds us that leveraging the Internet in the 21st century is as critical to the company's future success as pioneering the moving assembly line was to our success in the previous one. Bipen Patel—Director Management Systems—Ford (www.documentum.com, accessed March 11, 2019)."

The Internet is a benefit to both large and small organizations. For large firms whose employees are not co-located, it permits vastly improved communication among its staff. For small to medium-sized organizations who need to support a worldwide customer base or wish to expand their reach the Internet is essential. The Internet is also impacting legal practices. "The way in which law firms are providing services is changing," said Knapp. "Clients are starting to expect the accessibility and collaborative features provided by portal solutions like Hummingbird Portal (www.hummingbird.com, accessed November 26, 2018)."

As more and more commerce is either taking place directly online and as off-line commerce is supported by Web sites that provide customers with all kinds of information, from product support to the location of dealers, the importance of the Internet to business grows day by day. The hyperlinking of information through the use of intranets and groupware, is also essential for the organization of a company's activities for a diverse number of functions, including the internal communication and the coordination required to conduct business, as well as for information sharing, knowledge management, budgeting, planning, product development and support. There is no doubt that the Internet is having a major impact on business particularly as new tools are developed. Jim Mitnick, Senior VP of Turner Construction and the creator of a knowledge network for his company credits Internet technology with a number of successes at his company. He said, "we saw a combination of knowledge management and online learning as the strategy that would facilitate our growth and enable us to develop the most highly informed workers in the construction industry (https://www.opentext.com/about/press-releases?id=1340, accessed January 24, 2021)."

Internet Culture

Media guru Marshall McLuhan, who never actually experienced the Internet, had a number of insights about the nature of electric information that have turned out to be an accurate description of the effects of the Internet.

> The medium, or process, of our time—electric technology—is reshaping and restructuring patterns of social interdependence and every aspect of our personal life. It is forcing us to reconsider and re-evaluate practically every thought, every action and every institution formerly taken for granted — you, your family, your neighborhood, your education, your job, your government, your relation to "the others. And they're changing dramatically (McLuhan with Fiore 1967; also available at https://www.themediumisthemassage.com/the-medium-or-process-of-our-time-electric-technology-is-reshaping-and-restructuring-patterns-of-social-interdependence-and-every-aspect-of-our-personal-life-it-is-forcing/, accessed January 29, 2021).

During the pre-Internet era information and knowledge were protected and treated as a private good. Happily, the spirit of the greater sharing knowledge developed naturally in the Internet/Web environment without any overall direction or management from any quarter. The World Wide Web, in fact, as its original architect, Tim Berners-Lee (1999, 99) declared, was designed for the free exchange of information:

> Whether inspired by free-market desires or humanistic ideals, we all felt that control was the wrong perspective. I think it's clear that I had designed the Web so there should

be no centralized place where someone would have to 'register' a new server or get approval of its contents. Philosophically, if the Web was to be a universal resource, it had to be able to grow in an unlimited way. Technically, if there was any centralized point of control, it would rapidly become a bottleneck that restricted the Web's growth, and the Web would never scale up. It being out of control was very important.

The Impact of the Internet

The Web together with the Internet has impacted almost every aspect of human endeavour for its more than 4.95 billion users including the access and storage of information, communication, entertainment, as well as the nature of work, business, commerce, government, politics, education, warfare, terrorism and social media. The remainder of this chapter will be devoted to the impact of the Net and the Web, which have had a profound effect on each of these activities. We will, however, defer our treatment of social media, the applications that have come to dominate the Web to the later chapters of this book.

The Access and Storage of Information

The Web also provides the surfer with access to hordes of information including dictionaries; encyclopedias; almanacs; catalogs; course descriptions and content; newspapers, magazines and academic journal articles; collections of information about a myriad of subjects including the accomplishments of scholars, artists, writers, performers, television and movie stars, and politicians, as well as various hobbies, past times, sports, games, histories, geographies, sciences, social sciences, etc., etc.

The content of the Web includes recordings, radio and television shows, journal articles, newspaper stories, encyclopedias, dictionaries, etc. illustrating that the content of a new medium is always some older medium or media. "The new environment reprocesses the old one (McLuhan 1964, vii)."

The Internet is the world's largest library of stored information including information that was originally in a digital or even an analog format. "The main characteristic of the storage trajectory is the digitalization of previously analog information [from 0.8% digital in 1986 to 94% in 2007] (Hilbert & Lopez 2011)." The catalogue for the library that is the Internet are the search engines of which Google is the most dominant with 91.54% market share followed by Bing at 2.44%, Yahoo at 1.64% and Baidu (Chinese searches) at 1.08% respectively of market share (https://www.webfx.com/blog/seo/2019-search-market-share/, accessed January 29, 2021).

Other prominent sources of Internet-based information include:

- The Gutenberg Project that offers over 57,000 free eBooks;
- Wikipedia, a multilingual, web-based, free-content encyclopedia that is based on a model of openly editable content;
- Encyclopedia Britannica by subscription
- Online encyclopedias—On https://en.wikipedia.org/wiki/List_of_online_encyclopedias (accessed June 30, 2020) there is a list of 189 online encyclopedias in many different languages and on many different topics.
- The Way Back Machine (https://archive.org/web/) archives almost all Web sites dating back to the origin of the World Wide Web
- The Cloud is an interconnect network of servers that stores the contents of millions of personal computers that are only accessible to the particular personal computer that stored its data on the Cloud.

The Internet, the Web and Entertainment

The Web through the transmission capability of the Internet became a global network for the transmission of ideas, articles, music, visual arts, movies, television and radio shows, the sharing of videos through YouTube, Vimeo and other similar apps.

The Internet and Communication

The Internet facilitates communication between agents in real time through visual telephoning through apps like Skype or Viber, online meetings among participants from all over the globe through apps like GoToMeeting, Google Hangout and Zoom. These apps became critical to so many activities during the Covid-19 pandemic.

The Internet and Its Impact on Work

The nature of office work has changed due to the automating of so many functions such as correspondence, invoicing and collecting, inventory management, scheduling, procurement, internal communication and coordination, etc., etc. Telecommuting has changed where workers carry out their work functions with some able to work from home instead of coming to their office every day. Telecommuting became a critical tool that allowed many organizations to carry on their activities during the Covid-19 pandemic.

The Internet and Its Impact on Commerce and Business

More and more retail transactions are carried out online with companies like Amazon delivering what their customers order through the postal service or through private couriers. Amazon which began with books now carries a wide variety of products and even some services such as Cloud services. Some on-line retailers specialize in a narrow product line like Wayfair which specializes in furniture.

According to https://www.statista.com/statistics/379046/worldwide-retail-e-commerce-sales/ (accessed June 30, 2020) retail e-commerce world-wide was at $US 3.54 trillion in 2019 (representing 9% of all retail sales world-wide) up from $US 2.98 trillion in 2018 and projected to hit $US 6.54 trillion in 2022.

The Internet and Its Impact on Government

Federal, state or provincial and municipal governments provide services to their citizens online such as the renewal of drivers' licenses, license plates, health cards and passports.

References

Berners-Lee, Tim. 1999. *Weaving the Web*. San Francisco: Harper.

Gibson, William. 1984. *Neuromancer*. New York: Ace Books.

Hilbert, Martin, and Priscila Lopez. 2011. "The World's Technological Capacity to Store, Communicate, and Compute Information." *Science* 332: 60–65.

McLuhan, Marshall. 1964. *Understanding Media: Extensions of Man*. New York: McGraw Hill. (The page references in the text are for the McGraw Hill paperback second edition. Readers should be aware that the pagination in other editions is different.)

McLuhan, Marshall. 1995. "I. About Media." In *Essential McLuhan*, edited by Eric McLuhan and Frank Zingrone. Concord Ontario: Anansi.

Nelson, Theodor. 1965. "Complex Information Processing: A File Structure for the Complex, the Changing and the Indeterminate." In *Proceeding ACM '65 Proceedings of the 1965 20th National Conference*, 84–100. New York: ACM.

Nelson, Theodor. 1974. Computer Lib: You Can and Must Understand Computers Now/Dream Machines: New Freedoms Through Computer Screens—A Minority Report (1st ed.; 2nd ed. 1987). Redmond, WA: Tempus Books of Microsoft Press.

Nelson, Theodor. 1987. Computer Lib: *You Can and Must Understand Computers Now/Dream Machines: New Freedoms Through Computer Screens* (Rev. ed.). Redmond, WA: Tempus Books of Microsoft Press.

CHAPTER FOUR

Impacts of the Smartphone and Their Apps

LOM: The Smartphone

Enhances: the mobility of access to the Internet and telephone communication;
Obsolesces: the cell phone and the landline;
Retrieves: nomadic existence;
Reverses or flips into: obsession, loss of contact with the real world and a lack of privacy.

History of Mobile Phones and Its Evolution into the Smartphone

The story of the smartphone begins with the invention of the telephone and then the mobile phone. The first version of mobile phones were car phones which were radio-based telephones that allowed mobile telephone communication within the confines of one's automobile. They first appeared in 1946 using equipment developed by Motorola and were used on the Bell Telephone service as early as 1946.

The second version of mobile phones were cordless telephones using the regular telephone infrastructure but in which a radio signal from the cordless telephones communicated with the docking station of the cordless telephone, which in turn is connected with the regular telephone network. They were first developed and commercialized in the mid to late 1960s but the area of mobility was limited to the distance at which the cordless phone could communicate with the docking station, which was the living or working space of the user.

The first truly mobile portable hand-held phone was invented by Dr. Martin Cooper, a researcher at Motorola in 1973. He made the first mobile phone call that did not originate in an automobile. It was not until 1983, however, that portable hand-held phones were available for use by the public. These first devices were manufactured by Motorola.

In 1993 IBM introduced what might be considered the first smartphone the Simon which had the capability of a mobile phone, a pager, a fax machine and a Personal Digital Assistant (PDA) with a calendar, address book, clock, calculator, notepad, email, fax and a touchscreen with a QWERTY keyboard (https://en.wikipedia.org/wiki/History_of_mobile_phones#cite_note-Techblog-38 accessed on October 21, 2018). It was available commercially a year later and marketed as the Simon Personal Communicator without the use of the term smartphone, which was only introduced in 1995 to describe AT&T's PhoneWriter Communicator.

The first camera phones began to appear around 2000 with Sharp's J-Phone in Japan and with Samsung's SCH-V200 in Korea. They did not hit the North American market until 2004.

The first smartphone, in the modern sense of the term, with access to Wi-Fi and a keypad appeared in 2003 developed and marketed by Research in Motion (RIM, now Blackberry Ltd.). RIM as early as 1999 had created a two-way pager with a keypad, which was a unique feature of its time.

> In 2003 BlackBerry introduced the first of what we would think of as being the modern smart phone. This was a device that not only functioned as a telephone but also allowed for the sending and receiving of email and text messages as well as web browsing. One of the main focuses of the early BlackBerry's was to allow for mobile email (http://www.bbscnw.com/a-short-history-of-the-blackberry.php, accessed on October 21, 2018).

The next jump in the evolution of the smartphone came with the release of Apple's iPhone in 2007, a mobile phone with access to the Internet, a touch sensitive screen and all the features of the iPod, a portable media player and a multi-purpose pocket computer. The age of the smartphone was now in full gear. As time passed the technology improved, the number of users increased and new producers appeared using Google's Android operating system. Among the leaders of Android smartphones are Samsung from Korea and Huawei and Xiaomi from

China. Apple that once dominated the smartphone market is now ranked third behind Samsung and Huawei in terms of the number of units sold each year.

It is worth noting that the inevitability of the smart phone was something that Marshall McLuhan foreshadowed in the mid 1960s as was described by his biographer Phillip Marchand (1989, 170). "He told an audience in New York City shortly after the publication of *Understanding Media* that there might come a day when we would all have portable computers, about the size of a hearing aid, to help mesh our personal experiences with the experience of the great wired brain of the outer world." By the way, a hearing aid back in the day when McLuhan made his prediction was much larger and about the size of today's smart phones. What makes his prediction so extraordinary is that when he made it there were no personal computers, no cell phones and no Internet, i.e. "the great wired brain of the outer world (ibid.)".

Mobile Technology, The Medium of Media

Smartphones are the dominant digital media of today. In 2020, the number of smartphone users in the world is 3.5 Billion, which translates to 44.98% of the world's population owning a smartphone and 4.78 Billion users of mobile phones or 61.43% of the world's population (https://www.bankmycell.com/blog/how-many-phones-are-in-the-world, accessed June 30, 2020). The Asia-Pacific region accounts for more than half of the smartphone users.

Just as we asserted in the last chapter that the content of any medium is another medium, the content of the smartphone is a medium of media providing many applications or functions including accessing the Internet and the World Wide Web, texting, telephoning, taking photos, shooting videos, scanning, photocopying (when connected to a printer), using it as: a gaming station, a video player, an e-reader, a hailer of taxis or Uber, a translator, a calendar, a note taker, a clock, a stop watch, a scientific calculator, a music player, a voice recorder of lectures, meetings and interviews. And then there is of course all the apps that have been downloaded on to the smartphone such as a long list of social media.

The smart phone is a hybrid technology that combines the cell phone with all of the features of a computer connected to wi-fi and then some (many of the items in this list were found on the site: https://www.goconqr.com/en/examtime/blog/40-uses-for-smartphones-in-school/, accessed June 30, 2020). The smartphone is a hybrid technology and as McLuhan (1964, 55) noted, "The hybrid or the meeting of two media is a moment of truth and revelation from which new form is born." That certainly is the case with the smartphone.

The Co-Evolution of Smart Phones and Their Users

Marshall McLuhan claims that media are an extension of man, which is certainly the case with the smartphone. Since the rise of the smartphone, tech users have continued to update their iOS, Android or Blackberry devices throughout the many versions and purchased new smartphone models as they come out year after year. Although the smartphone's physical attributes and features have evolved and changed in design, accessibility, and model, the data accumulated by each user has remained in-tact throughout the various upgrades thanks to the Cloud. In a way, individuals have grown up and evolved as their smartphones have. It is also the case that our digital media such as the smartphone, our personal computers, our tablets etc. etc. have mirrored our own growth having evolved new features and capabilities. A part of everyone's personality and life experiences are stored on their smart phones; including their online personas, their personal data, their private information, their memories, etc. etc.

How Smartphones Hijacked Our Minds

No digital device is more ubiquitous than the smartphone. They are everywhere never more than inches from their owners who are for the most part totally addicted to them and absorb more of the attention of their users waking hours than any other activity. The title to this section and its content was inspired by an article by Haley Sweetland Edwards (2018) entitled: "You're Addicted to Your Smartphone. This Company Thinks It Can Change That." The article discusses the work of an organization Boundless Mind founded by two young neuroscientists, Ramsay Brown and T. Dalton Combs, who want "to disrupt America's addiction to technology" using the same tools that make social media so habit forming.

> It used to be that pathogens and cars were killing us. Now it's cheeseburgers and social media. It's our habits and addictions. Every day, we check our phones an average of 47 times–every 19 minutes of our waking lives–and spend roughly five hours total peering at their silvery glow. There's no good consensus about what all this screen time means for children's brains, adolescents' moods or the future of our democratic institutions. But many of us are seized these days with a feeling that it's not good. Last year, the American Psychological Association found that 65% of us believe that periodically unplugging would improve our mental health, and a 2017 University of Texas study found that the mere presence of our smartphones, face down on the desk in front of us, undercuts our ability to perform basic cognitive tasks. New York University

psychologist Adam Alter describes the current state of tech obsession as a "full-blown epidemic" (ibid.).

Brown and Combs are sympathetic to this backlash, but they're also deeply skeptical of the proposed solutions.

"We're not getting rid of this stuff–there's no way," Brown says. "No piece of technology, once adopted, ever gets put back in the box." Instead, he and Combs propose a different tactic, born of the relentless optimism of Silicon Valley: fight fire with fire. Why not harness those same, powerful persuasive technologies that Big Tech has in its arsenal but, instead of deploying them to maximize eyeball time, use them to promote a healthy, democratic society (ibid.)?

Here are some revealing facts from www.socialmediatoday/news/smartphone-etiquette-2018-infographic/531993 (accessed June 30, 2020) that back up Brown and Combs concerns and show that smart phones steal our time as they are great time wasters:

- 92% of Americans believe smartphone addiction is real.
- 43% of millennials check their phone at least every 20 minutes.
- 60% think they touch their phones 100 times or less per day versus a typical user taps, touches or swipes their phone 2,617 times per day.
- 20% check their phone every 20 minutes; 14% every 30 minutes; 25% every hour; 19% every 2–3 hours; 10% every 3–5 hours; 10% about twice a day; and 2% never put it down.
- 70% say it's inappropriate to have a smartphone out during a meeting; but 53% do it anyway.
- 80% say it's inappropriate to check their phone during a meeting; but 50% do it anyway.
- 10% have had their phone out during an interview
- 77% bring their phone into the bathroom at work.

A measure of the obsession with smartphones is a product that has been developed by Marc Teyssier in France. The Mobilimb Finger is a touch-sensitive robotic finger that can be attached to smartphones that can crawl across the desk, waggle for attention when messages arrive and be used as an interface to control apps and games (http://newsvideo.su/video/9492927 accessed October 16, 2018).

Many people have dispensed with land-lines (non-mobile phones) and only depend on their smartphone for telephoning. And even then, the use of the phone to transmit live voice communication is not what it used to be. Instead of talking over a phone people are relying more and more on texting, chat apps and email to communicate. This is particularly true of young people like co-author Mira R., who grew up with texting and email. It is only older folks like co-author Bob L. who still enjoy schmoozing on the telephone, which, he believes, has the advantage that complicated or complex issues can be resolved more quickly in real time with a telephone conversation than in a series of back and forth emails stretched over time.

Health Issues with the Extensive or Excessive Use of Smartphones or Cell Phones

A video posted on https://www.self.com/video/watch/common-health-issues-caused-by-phones, accessed June 30, 2020 documents some of the health issues that occur with the extensive or excessive use of smartphones or cell phones:

> Prolonged cell phone use can cause health issues like neck pains, dry eyes and a numb thumb. Here are four common phone-related issues and how to prevent each one.

1. Tech neck occurs when your neck isn't aligned properly when you use your phone, the muscles in your neck can tighten which can cause headaches and pain radiating from your shoulders. Try keeping your phone at eye level and limit the time you spend using it.
2. Numb thumb. Carpal tunnel syndrome could be causing that burning or tingly numbness near your thumb. This happens when the median nerve in your hand's carpal tunnel becomes pinched. Get a grip for the back of your phone to prop it upon a surface so you can tap out your texts. Make sure to stretch your wrists and fingers regularly.
3. Cell phone elbow. Cell phone elbow happens when the ulnar nerve that connects through your neck, elbow, and hand gets compressed. This creates aching or numbness around your elbow, down your arm into your pinky and ring fingers. If you frequently use your phone, switch hands often or use a hands-free headset. You can also extend your arms straight behind your body and flex your elbows.
4. Dry eyes. When you blink, your eyes produce tears to make them hydrated. Staring at a screen for long periods of time makes you blink less, which creates burning, dryness, or redness. Try the 20–20–20 rule: take a 20-second break from your phone to look at something 20 feet away every 20 minutes.

A measure of smartphone addiction is that their use does not end with the waking day. Many users bring their devices with them to bed and use them just before falling asleep and/or the first thing when awaking in the morning. Studies have shown that the practice of using the smartphone just before going to sleep degrades the quality of the sleep of those that use their smartphone right up to the last minute just before falling asleep.

> Seventy-one percent of people sleep either holding their smartphone, having it in bed with them, or having it on their nightstand [using it just before going to sleep] … Smartphones … emit something called blue light, which is a type of light that the brain interprets as daylight. The blue light actually suppresses melatonin (a hormone that affects circadian rhythm and should increase when you are preparing for bedtime). The result: Your brain feels stimulated [and] is going to get confused and think that the sun is out—making it even tougher to fall asleep (https://www.sleep.org/articles/is-your-smartphone-ruining-your-sleep/, accessed June 30, 2020).

It has been recently reported by researchers at Villanova University's M. Louise Fitzpatrick College of Nursing that not only are smartphones used just before falling asleep and just upon awaking but also while the smartphone user is actually asleep in what is called "sleep texting." "One student said she wears mittens to bed every night to prevent texting since 'moving the phone from being in my bed to next to the bed is not an option, I have to keep my phone with me' (https://www.huffingtonpost.ca/2018/11/28/sleep-texting-teens_a_23603640/ accessed Nov. 29, 2018)."

Smartphones and Mindfulness

A recent study published in *Cyberpsychology, Behavior, and Social Networking* and reported in *Psychology Today* (https://www.psychologytoday.com/intl/blog/urban-survival/201812/study-finds-being-your-phone-constantly-can-be-harmful?fbcl id=IwAR0KK1D0UEHXwUFZEO5veZGy8ePs2tDhwKniIN4ei2kSw86Xnv_ n5nPKf3A accessed on December 15, 2018) indicates that being plugged into one's smartphone and constantly checking it for messages results in users being distracted and preoccupied resulting in a loss of mindfulness. Smartphone obsession gives rise to anxiety waiting for replies to previous messages. It also distracts the user when engaged in social activities and/or work activity.

Could Smartphone Addiction Become Even Greater

In a report posted March 4, 2018 in the German news magazine Der Spiegel it was reported that certain Silicon Valley optimists are suggesting that in the future there will be an an even more pervasive use mobile technology, one that is non-stop.

How Silicon Valley Shapes Our Future

> Smartphones are being improved at intervals of decreasing length. In another 25 years, say techies from the Valley, we won't have to carry devices with us at all anymore. They will be replaced by molecular computers and biometric sensors that are woven into the world around us (http://www.spiegel.de/international/germany/ spiegel-cover-story-how-silicon-valley-shapes-our-future-a-1021557.html accessed on March 7, 2018).

Shortly after the appearance of this article, the Canadian start-up company, North Inc. (formerly Thalmic Labs), based in Kitchener Ontario announced on October 23, 2018 the release of its new product Focals, which allows one to be in constant touch with one's incoming messages as suggested in the Der Spiegel article above. Focals are not "molecular computers and biometric sensors," but rather a wearable technology, namely smart glasses.

Focals is a form of mobile technology in which the lens project holographic images into the retina allowing the wearer to see their latest emails, notifications and text messages. Focals is controlled by voice commands and also a ring one wears on the index finger of one's right hand with a button that acts as a joystick. Swiping either left or right allows one to swipe through one's messages and pushing down of the button allows one to select the message one wishes to access.

While Focals is not a smart phone but it shares many common features of a smartphone in the sense that it delivers information to its users. It does not, however, have any of the iPod features of an iPhone or android devices. But it does have built into it the feature of Amazon's Alexa assistant which can be activated by voice and whose voice messages can be heard by the built-in speakers of the device.

North Inc. believes that Focals will succeed because unlike Google Glasses it does not take make photo or videos which was a feature that many non-users of Google Glasses objected to. They are also quite stylish, designed by a well-known designer of eyeglass frames. They look like a regular pair of eye glasses unlike Google Glasses with their obtrusive camera on the corner of the right lens. Here is a picture of a typical user of Focals wearing the smart eye glasses and the black ring which acts as a controller of the device. The model happens to be Natalie Logan, who worked at North Inc. on the Focals project as an advance research and development specialist. By coincidence she is also the daughter of one of the co-authors of this book (RKL).

The Revival of Dumbphones: Countering Smartphone Addiction

The dumbphone is just a mobile telephone without any connection to the Internet and serves only two purposes (1) the reception and the initiation of voice only telephone conversations and (2) texting. With the popularity of smartphones, it was believed that the dumbphone would become extinct and disappear. The year 2013 was the year that smartphones sales topped dumbphone sales and it was when the complete demise of the dumbphone was predicted. Well the reports of the death of the dumbphone like that of Mark Twain's death turn out to have been greatly exaggerated. The dumbphone is alive and well. In fact, according to the research firm Gartner nearly 400 million dumbphones were sold in 2016 compared to 1.5 billion smartphones (https://www.thestar.com.my/tech/tech-news/2017/02/27/dumbphones-survive-rise-of-the-smartphone/ accessed January 3, 2019).

One of the key advantages of dumbphones is that they are affordable which explains why they outsell smartphones in emerging markets like India. Another advantage is that they can be used in areas where access to Wi-Fi is limited or non-existent. Another reason for the popularity of the dumbphone in developing countries is understandable because of the expense of a smart phone but there is a revival of dumbphones being promoted in markets to people who can afford a smart phone but choose to liberate themselves from their smartphone. First, there are the older folks who are just not into email and want to have an affordable mobile telephone connection. But the surprise is that a market for dumbphones is emerging in the developed countries among a group of consumers known as smartphone refuseniks. They find that the constant stream of emails distracting with the effect that they reduce the quality of their social life and their interaction with their family members especially their young children.

Rabbi Elchanan Shoff who engages in counseling members of his congregation who are in need finds that his dumbphone lets him stay focused. He reports that, "it allows me to get things done professionally and not always be on immediate call for people. I don't see emails for hours, and I am able to reply when it's convenient and focus on the task at hand without the constant distraction of connectivity (https://www.wework.com/creator/work-life-balance/why-some-people-are-dumbing-down-their-phones/ accessed January 3, 2019.)" Some former smart phone users switched to dumbphones because it was the only way to deal with their smartphone addiction. One such addict reported, "Some people drink too much; I spent too much time scrolling aimlessly through my friends' updates, taking pictures of my food instead of enjoying it, and consuming content instead of creating it (ibid.)."

These folks are content with a mobile telephone that can be used as a portable phone for voiced communication but also can be used to receive and dispatch text messages. To meet this new demand Nokia released a revamped version of its iconic 3310 model that had not been manufactured more than a decade after it was discontinued. In addition, some new models of mobile phones have emerged on the market which are not quite classical dumbphones because they have a few additional features like a smartphone but they are limited. John Pavlus (2019) describes this development in the following terms,

> Luckily, a small cottage industry has sprung up within the past several years to get you off your smartphone by actually replacing the physical device itself. Punkt, Palm, Light–these hardware start-ups are all relying on thoughtful-but-aggressive design to accomplish one goal: unplugging you from the Distraction Industrial Complex without turning you into a mobile-tech Luddite in the process.

The Light Phone 2 which sells for US$300 promotes itself by saying it is designed to be used as little as possible. The Light Phone II is a simple, 4G LTE phone with a beautiful black & white matte E-ink display. The Light Phone II brings a few essential tools, like messaging and an alarm clock, so it's even easier to ditch your smartphone more often, or for good. It's a phone that actually respects you (https://www.thelightphone.com/#lpii, accessed January 10, 2018).

The Palm Phone is a companion phone to one's smartphone on the Verizon network selling for US$349. It has the same phone number as its smartphone companion. It allows you to take this tiny compact smart phone with you where mobility is required and leave your much larger smartphone at home. Verizon promotes it by saying: "When you need to simplify. Whether you're on the go or in the moment, Palm lets you slim down and connect to what matters – easily (www.verizon.com/about/devices/palm/, accessed January 11, 2019)."

The Punkt MP02 out of Switzerland promotes itself by saying: "Looking for balance? Here it comes. The best of both worlds (https://www.punkt.ch/en/products/mp02-4g-mobile-phone/, accessed January 11, 2019)." It is a classical dumbphone that allows one to talk and text with one additional smart feature, namely, it can be used to allow your laptop computer or tablet to go online should you find yourself with no hot spot readily available. The MP02 is small and light and fits easily into a pocket. It also has the additional feature that it provides a Blackberry level of security, the only non-Blackberry phone to do so.

References

Edwards, Haley Sweetland. 2018. "You're Addicted to Your Smartphone. This Company Thinks It Can Change that http://time.com/5237434/youre-addicted-to-your-smartphone-this-company-thinks-it-can-change-that/. Accessed October 5, 2016."

Marchand, Phillip. 1989. *Marshall McLuhan: The Medium and the Messenger*. Toronto: Random House.

McLuhan, Marshall. 1964. *Understanding Media: Extensions of Man*. New York: McGraw Hill. (The page references in the text are for the McGraw Hill paperback second edition. Readers should be aware that the pagination in other editions is different.)

Pavlus, John. 2019. "This Device Is an Open Rebellion Against Everything that Smartphones Have Become." https://www.fastcompany.com/90290440/what-happened-when-i-replaced-my-iphone-with-a-dumbphone-for-a-week/. Accessed May 17, 20021.

CHAPTER FIVE

Online Communication Channels: E-mail, IM, Texting, VoIP, and Online Meeting Apps

LOM: Online Communication Channels

Enhance: personal communication, planning or scheduling;
Obsolesce: phone calls, letters, snail mail, fax, greeting cards, formal invitations;
Retrieve: postal service, telephone, telegrams and the town crier;
Reverse or flip into: spam with email, information overload, a time waster.

Introduction

In this chapter we will review the online communication channels that are part of the social media ecosystem just as we reviewed in the previous chapters the role and contribution of computing, the Internet, the Web and smartphones. The specific channels we will survey include email, instant messaging (IM), texting, VoIP (voice over IP) and group meeting apps. Missing from this list is Twitter, which is technically a communication channel but so are all social media in the sense that one can leave comments, likes and other messages. We shall treat Twitter (in Chapter Fifteen) as a social media app because all the communications of an account are generated by a single individual and hence reflects the personality and the persona of the tweeter just like standard social media apps like Facebook or

Instagram does for those that post using these apps. We have also classified You Tube as a social media app rather than a communication channel for the same reason.

E-mail, IM, and Texting

LOM: Email, IM and SMS

Enhance: personal communication,
Obsolesce: fax, personal letters
Retrieve: the postal service, and
Reverse and flip into: spam.

Email, instant messaging (IM), texting (short message service or SMS) and VoIP (voice over IP to be discussed in the next section of this chapter) are forms of social media that take advantage of digital technology by facilitating communication between friends, family, acquaintances and colleagues. They differ from standard social media like Facebook and Instagram in that they do not involve posting information about their users. They are strictly about communication. They have almost totally replaced personal letter writing. For the most part, the only letters that go through the postal system, known as snail mail, are legal documents and bills. They have also reduced the number of voiced telephone calls. Email, IM and VoIP are transmitted by the Internet whereas texting is exclusively sent via cell phones. Email and IM also differ from texting in that they are asynchronous. Another difference is that IM and texting are ephemeral as no record is made of these communications and as a result they disappear like oral communication. Email messages, on the other hand, are archived and often saved for future reference unlike texting and instant messaging. VoIP conversations can be archived but are for the most part not saved.

Texting, IM and VoIP are used primarily for one to one communication between the sender and the receiver. They can also be structured as a group chat with multiple people. Email, however, can be used to asynchronously message one person or a group of people with a text-based message with or without attachments. That is another difference as texting and IM do not involve attachments, but they can include hyperlinks which basically provide the same functionality as an attachment. Email attachments can be text files, graphics and/or videos. Email is also the medium for a listserv, whose email messages are posted by an individual to all the members on the listserv simultaneously. The posts often prompt a series of responses with the same subject heading, which is known as a thread. The individuals on a particular listserv share a common interest, which is the focus of the listserv. A listserv typically has a few people who make numerous posts, some that make occasional posts and some that are lurkers, who do not post but just read the listserv posting of others without commenting.

The forerunners of email, IM and texting were the telegraph, Telex and fax as they were the first ways of sending text messages electrically or electronically. The actual first forms of email emerged with the advent of time-sharing computers in the early 1960s but there were no universal protocols and hence the different email apps were incompatible. With Arpanet and then the Internet the transmission of email became standardized through the implementation of the following email protocols: SMTP (Simple Mail Transfer Protocol), POP (Post Office Protocol) and IMAP (Internet Message Access Protocol). As with email IM had a pre-Internet existence with local protocols but now IM operates using XMPP (Extensible Messaging and Presence Protocol).

Texting or text messaging involves sending short, alphanumeric messages between cellphone or pager users as implemented by a wireless carrier. It has been described as text-based voice mail.

Number of Users and Emails Sent Daily

There are approximately 3.9 billion users of email in the world or slightly more than half the world's population. The number of emails sent every year is approximately 294 billion with that number expected to continually rise with time (https://financesonline.com/number-of-email-users/, accessed March 6, 2020).

Tallying the number of IM users is difficult because there are so many providers of this service. Here are the number of subscribers or monthly users for a number of providers of these services as reported on Wikipedia: WhatsApp 2 billion, Skype 1.55 billion, WeChat 1.13 billion, Viber 1.1 billion, FB Messenger 900 million, Tencent 823 million, Kik Messenger 300 million, eBuddy 250 million, Line 217 million, Apple's iMessage 140 million, Snapchat 301 million monthly users, and Sharechat 60 million monthly users (https://en.wikipedia.org/wiki/Instant_messaging, accessed March 6, 2020). The number of IM users is not the sum of these numbers as many use multiple IM platforms.

Orality-Like Quality of Email, IM and Texting

Even though email, IM and texting are text-based they have an oral chatty character to them. They have this conversational quality to them because it is so easy to respond to them. Their messages tend to be transmitted with a minimum number of characters. They often make use of shorthand ways of spelling words so as to take advantage of phonetic cues. Thus, 'for you' for example can be represented as '4U'. Also, the proper grammatical syntax is often dispensed with in the interest of brevity. When one analyzes the attributes of email, IM or texting communications, it is apparent according to Naomi S. Baron (http://erhetoric.org/Erhetoric/wikka. php?wakka=BaronOnEmail, accessed on January 24, 2021) that the large majority of messages are characterized by the following three attributes:

- "informality of language style,
- psychological assumption that the medium is ephemeral
- high level of candor (stemming, at least in part, from treating email as an ephemeral medium)."

The relaxation of the strict rules of grammar with online messaging parallels the fact that in oral communication following the rules of grammar is often relaxed because there are other signals to carry meaning such as the mimetic signals of facial expression, hand signals, body language and tone. Grammar is absolutely necessary for written language because there are no mimetic signals to help convey the message of the writer. With online written language there are emojis to carry some extra meaning. Also, the online communication is conversational-like because of the ease of the receiver to responding quickly to clear up any ambiguities in the sender's message.

Email, IM and texting have by and large replaced faxes except in a situation where one wishes to transmit a hard copy document to a distant location without the delay of the postal system. With a fax one has to prepare a document in a hard copy format and then fax it. Whereas with email one can immediately respond using one's computer or smartphone. The normal patterns of usage of email is one in which one replies instantly to the message one has just received, which is what gives the medium its conversational quality. It is worth mentioning that younger users prefer IM and texting to email and the reverse is true for older users. Email, IM and texting allow text-based conversations to take place in real time just like a telephone conversation. The advantage of these media over a telephone conversation is the time lag between messages bouncing back between correspondents allows them to do other things.

The appeal of IM, in particular, is its multi-tasking capability. Teenagers often carry on multiple IM sessions at the same time. My daughters (RKL's) when they were teenagers reported that they could talk to four or five people at the same time via IM all the time carrying on a telephone conversation or doing homework. IM services typically feature a buddy list of contacts and indicate which people on the buddy list are currently online and available to chat. It is for these reasons that teenagers on the whole prefer IM over email.

Service and Disservice of Email, IM and Texting

Email, IM and texting provides an example of the service and disservice of technology that McLuhan (https://www.facebook.com/mcluhanestate/posts/ -the-message-as-it-relates-to-the-medium-is-never-the-content-but-the- corporate-/2295326123909867/, accessed August 26, 2020) suggested was true of all technologies. Service includes the fact that email facilitates billions of communications each day between individuals across the planet as well as in the same office. Email allows a flow of ideas, information and even dialogue without the frustrations of having to play telephone tag. Email, IM and texting provide control over space and time allowing us to increase the amount of communication we have with others in both business and social life. Email facilitates collaboration and sharing common interests for users that do not live in close proximity. Even for co-located email exchangers, email allows documents, images and videos to be conveniently exchanged. As one of us (RKL) who lived in the pre-email era can attest there is much more communication among friends and colleagues in the age of online communication and much more collaboration especially with those whom one does not have daily face-to-face contact. In RKL's research in the 31 years from 1965 to 1994, the year the Internet went public only 3 projects involved non-local colleagues. But in the 24 years from 1994 to 2020 there have been 26 projects involving non-local colleagues that's one a year in the digital age compared to one every 10 years in the pre-Internet era.

Email, IM or texting saves time as many messages can be sent without wasting time on the telephone or spending time coordinating a phone call among busy people. Also having a record of a communication can sometimes be very useful when there is a mix up in an organization. Another advantage of email, IM or texting is that it allows for group work without so many time-wasting inefficient meetings. Email is paperless but yet is archival.

On the disservice side of email is the plethora of spammed messages that clutter one's mailbox. Spam filters are not that effective in reducing the number of spammed messages that get through and many legitimate emails often wind up in the spam folder and so the spam folder also has to be monitored.

The speed-up of communication has both service and disservice.

> Email speeds up the exchange of information sometimes with disastrous effects. A Toronto lawyer and friend, reported that a number of his clients have gotten into trouble because they fired off emails without giving proper forethought to what they were saying and as a consequence compromised their positions. A hasty remark made in conversation cannot be recorded and held against a person in an oral negotiation, as is the case with a hasty email. A written response, on the other hand, is usually

carefully vetted before being sent out because the expectation of a rapid response time is not as great as is the case with email (Logan 2016, 252–53).

Another disservice of email in social interactions is that one tends to joke and banter with email in a way one would in conversation but not in a written communication. The problem of misinterpretation can easily arise because email does not provide the extra cues that spoken language carries as a result of tone, hand signals, body language, and facial gesture all of which are absent in email.

One harmful effect of email is phishing to gain access to information on one's computer that often leads to fraud of one kind or another. Perhaps the greatest disservice of email is that it is used to transmit computer viruses through email attachments. This has given rise to a whole industry to protect users from this insidious practice.

Email overload is another growing problem for many workers. Employees are sometimes so overwhelmed with catching up on email, they neglect other critical job duties. Email, IM and texting can interrupt one's time away from work by following one home and destroying the healthy division between work and private life. Email, IM and text messaging like written communication can be easily misinterpreted because of a lack of cues such as facial gestures and tone of voice. Emoji are sometimes used to fill in this gap.

VoIP (Voice over IP)

LOM: VoIP

Enhances: online communications by providing a visual link to voice communication; international employment opportunities; long distant relationships
Obsolesces: phone calls; in person interviews; travel for meetings
Retrieves: face-2-face meetings
Reverses or flips into: a meeting without the warmth of human contact

VoIP is literally voice over Internet Protocol (IP) is the delivery of voice and multi-media content over IP networks. The main advantage of VoIP is to allow the speakers of a VoIP session to see each other which is not possible with ordinary telephone conversations. Some applications of VoIP entail replacing traditional public switched telephone networks with VoIP to reduce the cost of telephony. VoIP also allows for group meetings. VoIP is a social medium in which the multi-media capabilities of VoIP connections are used to link individuals and create forums for connecting non-local users of computers, iPads or smartphones.

WhatsApp and Facebook Messenger

WhatsApp and Facebook Messenger are both owned by Facebook and provide similar services, namely, an instant messaging social media networking service for smartphones. They are both very popular because of their simplicity, instantaneous nature and ease of use. They both make use of VoIP so that a user can use the Internet to make video calls and voice calls; send messages, videos, images, documents and even audio files to another user or a group of users. Messenger also has the status feature where the user gets to upload videos and photos for a 24-hour timeline feed. These two Facebook apps have a combined user base of 2.8 billion users.

Skype and Viber

Skype, a subsidiary of Microsoft, provides VoIP services for computers, tablets and smartphones. Microsoft has integrated Skype with its other products. While not as popular as the Facebook VoIP products of WhatsApp and Messenger there are still many users of Skype. According to https://expandedramblings.com/index.php/skype-statistics/, accessed March 10, 2020, there are "300 million monthly users of Skype … it has been downloaded 1 billion times … and the total number of minutes spent on Skype per day is 3 billion."

Viber provides VoIP services for computers, tablets and smartphones like Skype but has a smaller market share but is popular "in Eastern Europe, Russia, the Middle East and some Asian markets (https://en.wikipedia.org/wiki/Viber, accessed March 10, 2020)."

Group Meeting Apps

While strictly not classified as social media the following group meeting apps do have a social dimension to them: Zoom, Google Hangouts, GoToMeeting, Join.me, Meetin.gs, Ready to Talk, Sync.in, Vyew, WebEx, Yugma, are worthy of mention. To this list we have added Meetup, a service used to organize online groups. Because of its ease of use Zoom has zoomed (pun intended) to popularity during the Covid pandemic allowing, for example, professors to deliver their lectures to their university students.

Conclusion: While email, IM, texting and VoIP are not strictly social media in the usual definition of the term, they are still digital media that play an important role of online social interactions.

Reference

Logan, Robert K. 2016. *Understanding New Media: Extending Marshall McLuhan*, 2nd edition, 252–53. New York: Peter Lang Publishing.

PART II

THE SOCIAL MEDIA REVOLUTION

CHAPTER SIX

The Impacts
of Social Media

LOM: Social Media

Enhance: social interactions online; connectivity beyond geographic boundaries;
Obsolesces: face-to-face interactions; selectivity in making friends;
Retrieves: lost connections; village life; a sense of community;
Reverses or flips into: fake identities; fake friendships; fake news; loss of meaningful relationships; misperceptions of others; loss of privacy; targeted advertising based on personal user data; browsing addiction.

Introduction

One of the major consequences of the Internet and the World Wide Web has been the emergence of social media. As of 2018 there were 2.65 billion social media users world-wide representing a 70% penetration rate of Internet users. The distribution of users with active accounts in billions, as of April 2018, for different applications is as follows: Facebook: 2.7 (i.e. 2.5 billion); YouTube: 2.0; WhatsApp: 2.0; Facebook Messenger: 1.3; WeChat: 1.206; Instagram: 1.158; TikTok: 0.689; QQ: 0.648; Douyin: 0.6; Sina Weibo: 0.523; QZone: 0.517; Reddit: 0.43; Kuiashou 0.4; Snapchat 0.398; Twitter: 0.386; Pinterest 0.366,

Douban 0.32; and Linkedin 0.310 (https://www.statista.com/statistics/272014/global-social-networks-ranked-by-number-of-users/, accessed January 11, 2021)

Social media are one of if not the most dominant class of applications on the Internet. In this chapter we will provide an overview of the phenomenon of social media leaving a description of individual social media sites to our next chapters.

McLuhan pointed out that all media provide both service and disservice when he wrote the following lines in an April 22, 1970 letter to Jonathan Miller: "All I am saying is that any product or innovation creates both service and disservice environments which reshape human attitudes. These service and disservice environments are always invisible until new environments have superseded them (Molinaro, McLuhan, & Toye 1987, 404)." It is our intention in this book to identify both the services and disservices of social media.

The popularity of social media sites as a communication platform by so many users is because they are used as a tool for the users to construct their identity and as the lens through which they perceive their world. This illustrates Marshall McLuhan's (1964) notion that media are an extension of their users that he formulated in his book, *Understanding Media: Extensions of Man*. Social media literally become an extension of their users. It is their eyes and ears on their social world. It is also the tool they use to create their online image, most often exaggerated and often fake because they edit their content to make themselves as attractive and as cool as possible. This is why social media become an extension of their users.

Social media discourage reading and thoughtfulness. Digital technologies promote multitasking because of the need to keep switching between apps, skim all media outlets, and thus absorb different forms of information. This exposes the users to brief highlights and disconnected chunks of information as opposed to detailed narratives.

The online social media listed above and a few others will be compared with real life social interactions. They will be discussed in accordance with the following media effects keeping in mind that all media have effects regardless of their content:

1. Real versus fake communication;
2. Thorough versus superficial content;
3. Social versus antisocial effects;
4. Mentally stimulating versus merely entertaining content; and
5. Objective communication versus propaganda and fake news.

Social media impact a number of different domains which we will entertain in our analysis. They include: the family; information media such as newspapers, radio and TV; social clubs; face-to-face conversations; schools and work; relationships; friendships; politics; and cultural life. Online social media are digital platforms that are constantly evolving just like the way Smartphones are constantly updated with new designs, features and tools. Social media play a big part in the way their users perceive the world and themselves, as they are often unconscious of the effects social media have on the construction of their identity, opinions, self-perception both online and in the real world. This further illustrates Marshall McLuhan's (1964) notion that media are extensions of their users.

Habit Forming Social Media

Social media are habit forming and addictive not just because people enjoy socializing online but because they have been designed to be so. One of the people who mastered the art of making social media addictive is Nir Eyal, the author of *Hooked: How to Build Habit-Forming Products* (Eyal 2013). He consulted with a number of social media firms teaching them the techniques to make their products addictive. He also conducted a workshop where participants could learn the techniques he developed for making the use of their apps compulsive. To protect his own family from the insidious effects of addictive Web sites and apps he installed in his home an "outlet timer connected to a router that cuts off access to the internet at a set time every day (P. Lewis 2017)."

Eyal defending his techniques against those that suggest digital addiction is similar to drug addiction wrote,

> We're not freebasing Facebook and injecting Instagram here … Just as we shouldn't blame the baker for making … delicious treats, we can't blame tech makers for making their products so good we want to use them. Of course, that's what tech companies will do. And frankly: do we want it any other way? (ibid.).

Our response to Eyal's question: "do we want it any other way?" is that the question is equivalent to asking a drug addict would they want their drugs to be less pleasurable. His remark begs the question. The maker and purveyor of a product or service is responsible for the harm their product or service creates. Just as laws were passed to make cigarettes less accessible, especially for teen agers, we suggest that at a minimum, purveyors of social media should at least self-regulate. There is a growing consensus that many social media companies are out of control and government regulation that does not violate the freedom of speech need to be seriously considered. We will return to this topic in the last chapter of this book.

Eyal was a student of B J Fogg (2002) who was the founder of the field of captology (a term Fogg coined). Fogg described captology in the following terms:

> After we ran a number of experiments, and after these studies were replicated else-where, the results were undeniable. Computers could indeed be designed to influence people, to change their thoughts and behaviours ... The feedback of the users of digital media become the feedforward for those media.

There is even an online newsletter, Social Media Today, that provides advice to social media marketers of how to make their social media campaigns more effective. An example of one of their articles is one entitled "6 Ways to Help Build Stronger Connection with Your Digital Communities (Lozano 2018)."

The motivation of creating addictive products is that social media companies make their living selling advertisements to their customers so that the more time users spend on their site the more money they earn. In the digital world it is the attention of the users that is monetized and hence the more addictive one can make one's site the more valuable it becomes. Social media firms are basically enslaving their users by capturing their attention and compensating them with the psychologically rewarding 'likes,' which are provided by other enslaved users. Another trick used by social media is to constantly alert its users every time a like or a friend's request arrives with a small red dot beside their app on their smart phone to grab the user's attention.

Millennials and Gen Z, who are especially heavy users of social media, are losing the skill of expressing themselves with written text. They prefer communicating with photos taken with their smart phones plus a few words of text often punctuated with emojis. No need to labour over putting some words together to describe their experiences since a picture, in their minds, is worth a thousand words. These users of social media especially millennials and Gen Z are losing the skills of literacy, both reading and writing. It is not that they cannot read and write, it is that they do not want to. They prefer reading short texts over reading a book. One day, while walking on the campus of the University of Toronto, I (RKL) overheard one student saying to another, "I actually read a book last week." He said it like it was a big accomplishment and something unusual to do.

In addition to not liking to read a long text like a book there is less of a need to read a book or a long essay as with Google one can easily find the information one is seeking using Google search or Google books where one can search for key words. Academic libraries also provide many articles in a digital format that can be easily searched obfuscating the need to read the entire article or book. This skimming of the literature is something that McLuhan did long before the digital revolution. He used to joke that he only read every other page because authors were so redundant. During an interview on CBC McLuhan said, "There is an enormous redundancy in every well-written book. With a well-written book, I only read the right-hand page and allow my mind to work on the left-hand page. With a poorly written book I read every word."

Awareness, Involvement and Detachment

In his review of Marshall McLuhan's book Understanding Media: Extensions of Man, Dennis Lewis's (1968) wrote,

> Awareness depends not only on involvement, but detachment as well. McLuhan himself points this out when he tells us that "when we want to get the bearings in our own culture and have the need to stand aside from the bias and pressure exerted by any technical form of human experience, we have only to visit a society where that particular form has not been felt, or a historical period in which it was unknown."

Lewis's (ibid.) observation that "awareness depends not only on involvement, but detachment as well," provides interesting insights into understanding why social media are so addictive from Marshall McLuhan's perspective of understanding the effects of media. One of the central themes of Marshall McLuhan's approach to understanding media and technology is that for the most part users are unaware of the subliminal effects of media. In *Understanding Media: Extensions of Man*, McLuhan (1964) wrote

> All technological extensions of ourselves must be numb and subliminal, else we could not endure the leverage exerted upon us by such extension. (McLuhan 1964, 264).

I am in the position of Louis Pasteur telling doctors that their greatest enemy was quite invisible, and quite unrecognized by them. Our conventional response to all media, namely that it is how they are used that counts, is the numb stance of the technological idiot (McLuhan 1964, 32).

It is the lack of detachment that prevents the ordinary users of a new technology from becoming aware of its effects. "Media effects are new environments as imperceptible as water to a fish, subliminal for the most part (McLuhan 1969, 22)." The users become so involved with this new extension of themselves that they are oblivious to its effects on them. The fish are involved with water but because they can never be detached from water they know nothing about water. The same is true of us with air. We are for the most part unaware of the air we breathe unless we are deprived of it, it becomes contaminated or it becomes stale and we feel the need for some fresh air.

Closely related to McLuhan's notion that the users of technology are unaware of the subliminal effects of their tools is the notion that because these tools are extensions of themselves they come to regard them as reflections of themselves and therefore relate to them as Narcissus did to his own reflection in the pond, falling in love with them. As Lewis (1968) points out because they are totally involved with their technologies they cannot detach themselves from these tools and hence are unaware of the impact these tools have on them. McLuhan describes this situation in the following poetic terms in *Understanding Media*:

> The Greek myth of Narcissus is directly concerned with a fact of human experience, as the word Narcissus indicates. It is from the Greek word narcosis, or numbness. The youth Narcissus mistook his own reflection in the water for another person. This extension of himself by mirror numbed his perceptions until he became the servomechanism of his own extended or repeated image. The nymph Echo tried to win his love with fragments of his own speech, but in vain. He was numb. He had adapted to his extension of himself and had become a closed system …

> To behold, use or perceive any extension of ourselves in technological form is necessarily to embrace it. To listen to radio or to read the printed page is to accept these extensions of ourselves into our personal system and to undergo the "closure" or displacement of perception that follows automatically. It is this continuous embrace of our own technology in daily use that puts us in the Narcissus role of subliminal awareness and numbness in relation to these images of ourselves. By continuously embracing technologies, we relate ourselves to them as servo-mechanisms. That is why we must, to use them at all, serve these objects, these extensions of ourselves, as gods or minor religions (McLuhan 1964, 51 & 55).

Lewis's (1968) notion that awareness depends not only on involvement, but detachment is an extremely deep idea that helps us understand why the users of social media are so deeply involved in these media that they are unaware of their effects. As Lewis points out the social media user is unaware of its effects because they are not detached from their social media. For them social media are part and parcel of their reality. They are attached to their social media at the hip as the saying goes and, in most cases, actually addicted to their attachment to social media. Social media are the most narcotic media.

Social media play a big part in the way their users perceive the world and themselves. Selfies with a celebrity is a form of fake news. In fact, almost all of social media is, in a certain sense, fake news. The most insidious form of fake news, however, is the pollution of mainstream news with phony narratives parading as genuine news disseminated by individuals, organizations and governments to sow dissention and hatred.

We Use Our Digital Media and They Use Us: The Flip from Media as Extensions of Man to Man as Extensions of Our Media

In addition to social media addiction there is another reason why social media is harmful and needs to be regulated. With digital media the users become extensions of their digital media as these media scoop up their data and use them to the advantage of those that control these media. The implication is our loss of privacy as we become "an item in a data bank (McLuhan and Powers 1989, 94)." The feedback of the users of digital media become the feedforward for those media.

As extensions of our digital technology the problem that arises is that because of the monopolies that digital media creates such as those of Google, Facebook, Instagram, Amazon, Yahoo, Twitter, Apple and Microsoft, the potential for their abuse is great. When our pre-digital technologies were only extensions of us they enhanced our capabilities and we were in command of them in the sense that they did our bidding as their servomechanisms. The tools no doubt affected us but they were not used by others to control us. That is no longer the case with digital media because those that control digital information systems can use the data we key into their systems to manipulate us. The field of captology, described above, has the direct aim of manipulating our behaviour by make use of what they learn about us as Fogg describes:

> Today, we are surrounded by persuasive technologies. Everywhere that digital media touches our lives, more and more there is an element of persuasion; a design created by humans and implemented in code to influence what we think, and more and more, what we do. We are surrounded. Persuasive technology is in our living rooms, in our cars. When we communicate with our loved ones online, through Facebook or Instagram, persuasion is there. When we withdraw money from the bank at the ATM, an element of persuasion may be there. When we purchase a gift online for a birthday, once again, we are being exposed to persuasion. In fact, we carry a persuasive platform, the mobile phone, with us most everywhere we go (http://captology.stanford.edu/re-sources/thoughts-onpersuasive-technology.html, accessed January 23, 2020).

The danger is that we are becoming an extension of our digital technologies. This in spite of the fact that on the surface the Internet gives us the illusion of being part of a two-way channel of communication. But the monopolies of the Internet that we listed above, to mention a few, dominate this medium of mediums. We are not suggesting that any of the organizations that we listed above have any malicious intents other than making as much money as possible. But still, when the concentration of computing power becomes so great the possibility of malevolent actions is something we need to think about. There is always a danger when control of the dominant technology of a culture is in the hands of a small number of players.

McLuhan (1964, 73) warned against this invasion of our privacy many years before digital media invaded our world when he wrote,

> Once we have surrendered our senses and nervous systems to the private manipulation of those who would try to benefit from taking a lease on our eyes and ears and nerves, we don't really have any rights left. Leasing our eyes and ears and nerves to commercial interests is like handing over the common speech to a private corporation, or like giving the earth's atmosphere to a company as a monopoly.

Ed Tywoniak, a media ecology professor emeritus at St. Mary's College in California (private communication) more recently pointed out "that the insidious aspect of digital technology is not that we interface with it but that it seeps into us and we are unaware of it."

Our relationship to media has changed because of the way in which the data we generate with the use of social media is, in turn, used by those very social media companies to enrich themselves at our expense. Marshall McLuhan (1964) in his book *Understanding Media: Extensions of Man* suggested that all of mankind's tools, technology or media are extensions of their users in the very title of that book. Our technologies, tools and media enhance our human functions and therefore they may be regarded as extensions of our being. McLuhan observed that mechanical technologies extended our bodies in space and that electric technology extended our central nervous system into what he termed "a global embrace, abolishing both space and time" (McLuhan 1964, 3). He wrote that, "all media are extensions of ourselves, or translations of some part of us into various materials (McLuhan 1964, 139)." Because of the way our data are used by the Internet monopolies, there is a flip from media as extensions of man as formulated by McLuhan in his book Understanding Media: Extensions of Man to humans as extensions of their digital media.

Other Negative Uses of Social Media

As with any medium, social media are also used for antisocial and even criminal activities. What makes social media a particularly dangerous medium for these negative uses of social media is that it so easy to disguise oneself online and to misrepresent oneself as belonging to an organization that the recipients of one's messages trust. In other words, social media, in particular, and online media, in general, are ideal media for committing fraud. Social media is also the ideal medium for fake news, the manipulation of political debates by agents domestic and foreign. It is used to spread hatred and the recruitment of terrorists by terrorist organizations.

It is worth noting that there are two kinds of fake news: (i) lies or made up story that are not true and (ii) credible stories that are true or mostly true and are labelled fake news because the news story is disliked by the person labelling them as fake news. Donald Trump, who made the term fake news au courant, traffics in both kinds making up stories on the social medium of Twitter that have no basis in fact and complaining about news coverage that he does not like labelling them fake news.

The unwise use of social media can lead to problems for their users. A number of people have lost their position because of hurtful, hateful or inappropriate things they have said on social media. Perhaps the most famous case is that of Roseanne Barr who lost her job starring on her hit television sitcom show 'Roseanne' after she posted a racist tweet attacking Valerie Jarrett, a former advisor to President Barrack Obama. Many other folks, less famous, also lost their jobs for unwise posts on social media for a variety of reasons for remarks including those that were lewd, racist, or too critical of their company or their boss. And then there were those that were not hired because of the offensive things they posted online. Whether its posting pictures, videos or that funny joke, the chances of your potential boss seeing it are likely. A new study from Career Builder reveals 70% of employers are checking out a candidate's social media profiles during the hiring process. (https://newyork.cbslocal.com/2018/09/19/hiring-process-social-media-career-builder-study, accessed July 13, 2019).

Other negative impacts of the use of social media include:

- Hacking in which personal information has led to negative consequences either social, financial or political for those that have been hacked.
- Cyberbullying, defined as "an aggressive, intentional act or behavior that is carried out by a group or an individual, using electronic forms of contact, repeatedly and over time against a victim who cannot easily defend him or herself (Moreno 2014)," has become a serious problem. It has tragically, led to an increasing number of suicides, especially among teenagers.
- Addiction to social media in which the user's face-to-face social media interactions become a substitute for actual face-to-face social interactions and companionship. A measure of the pervasiveness of social media addiction is the appearance of an article entitled "The Benefits of Taking A Social Media Break Are Worth Putting Your Phone Down For, Experts Say (Bissel 2018)." Among the benefits listed in this article, the one that caught our attention and tells the whole story of why social media addiction is so

harmful is the following: "You'll actually experience your own life (ibid.)." The implication is that many users/abusers of social media don't have a life because they are so involved with social media and their smartphones.

- Social media by glamorizing dangerous activities such as the use of drugs or alcohol or the performance life threatening stunts can encourage impressionable minds to follow suit with disastrous consequences.
- Social media generate Instagram envy or social media envy among visitors to sites that display what seems to be a perfect reality but what in reality is a fake or a manufactured reality. One example of the way images are faked is through the use of Facetune (https://www.facetuneapp.com), a photo editing app, that allows one to alter one's appearance so that they appear more attractive than they actually are in reality.

Roman Kordiuk, a Toronto-based high school teacher, who began his teaching career before the age of social media, has noticed that the social patterns of his students have changed with the arrival of smartphones and social media. Students spent considerably less time socializing face to face during breaks between classes because they are so busy texting. Somehow, a text seems more real than a spoken interchange. He also noticed that the consequences of bullying via social media, has more of a negative effect on his students, than was the case before the arrival of social media and smartphones, which he attributes to the fact that cyberbullying goes viral and includes so many more people.

Social media have created a false sense of success which is measured in terms of one's number of followers or the number of 'likes' one's post receives. One is reminded of what Nietzsche said about the vanity of having many followers, "What? You seek something? You wish to multiply yourself tenfold, a hundredfold? You seek followers? Seek zeros!"

The Positive Sides of Social Media

At the beginning of this chapter we said we would examine both the services and disservices of social media so in this section we turn to some of the positive aspects of social media. Probably the most important is that it gives a voice to anyone who can afford to go online which represents the overall majority of folks living in the developed and developing world.

Teenagers, ages 13–17, according to a study conducted by Common Sense Media, a San Francisco-based non-profit group, reported that "social media has a positive effect on their lives, helping them feel more confident, less lonely and less depressed (Ortutay 2018)." The same survey revealed that among American teens 44% use Snapchat, 22% Instagram and 15% Facebook. "Almost three-quarters of teens said they believe that tech companies manipulate people into spending more time on their devices and more than half said using social media often distracts them from homework."

Social media allow folks to contact friends and relatives with whom they have lost contact over the span of many years or with folks that have moved away.

Social media provide a medium for those who would not ordinarily have a voice to address the injustices they have endured.

Social media provide a medium for social and political activists or advocates of a noble cause to find like-minded souls to address the problems that exist in their society. During the American 2018 mid-term elections many celebrities used social media to persuade their followers to get out and vote.

Social media are used to keep indigenous cultures and languages to stay alive.

Social media is a way that help, both financial and material, can be directed to folks that have been victims of disasters of one kind or another.

People with a common problem or medical condition can and do support each other through social media. These forums help to inform or educate their users about their common problem or medical condition.

Social media also provide a medium for those that want to share information about their common interests or hobbies and hence to educate each other and also celebrate these activities.

Social media also provide a medium for small and medium-sized entrepreneurs to compete in the marketplace against big business. There are many artists that are able to make a living by offering their artistic creations for sale. There are also many small to medium sized online businesses that depend on social media to get their message out to potential customers.

Social Media as the Path to Stardom

Different media have given rise to different types of celebrities: oral media to bards and story tellers; written media to authors and philosophers; movies to movie stars; newspapers to those who were the subject of news coverage such as politicians, socialites, high ranking military officers, criminals, and the curious.

Social media have provided still another path to stardom. "In 2007, Bieber became the poster child of what social media can do when he was discovered by his manager, Scooter Braun, on YouTube (https://stylecaster.com/celebrities-discovered-on-social-media, accessed Jan 19, 2020)." Other examples of stars who got their start through YouTube include: Kate Upton whose "big break came when a friend posted a YouTube video of her doing the "dougie" at a basketball game in 2011 (ibid.)." The Weekend: aka, Abel Tesfaye, Alessia Cara, Troye Sivan, Tori Kelly, Madison Beer, and Darren Criss are all examples of vocalists who launched their career through YouTube. One exception is Colbie Caillat who launched her career through MySpace (ibid.). All of these examples are pop singers who became recognized through social media. But there are a whole host of other social media stars who are not just singers but comedians, film makers, gamers, fitness coaches, bloggers, who achieved stardom because of their social media presence on YouTube, Vine, Instagram, Google+, LinkedIn, Twitter, Tumblr and blogs in general. An extensive list of them can be found at (https://www.thefamouspeople.com/list-of-social-media-stars.php, accessed Jan 23, 2020).

Not all of the people who became famous through social media have elevated modern culture. One notorious example is Kim Kardashian whose road to celebrity came through the release of a sex tape. "Kardashian first gained media attention as a friend and stylist of Paris Hilton, but received wider notice after a 2003 sex tape with her former boyfriend Ray J was leaked in 2007. Later that year, she and her family began to appear in the E! reality television series Keeping Up with the Kardashians (https://en.wikipedia.org/wiki/Kim_Kardashian, accessed Jan 19, 2020)."

References

Bissel, Jordan. 2018. "The Benefits of Taking a Social Media Break Are Worth Putting Your Phone Down For, Experts Say" (https://www.elitedaily.com/p/3-mental-health-benefits-of-creativity-that-trump-how-intimidating-it-is-to-try-something-new-11858246, accessed September 26, 2018).

Eyal, Nir. 2013. *Hooked: How to Build Habit-Forming Products.* New York: Portfolio Penguin.

Fogg, B. J. 2002. *Persuasive Technology: Using Computers to Change What We Think and Do.* Burlington MA: Morgan Kaufmann.

Lewis, Dennis. 1968. "Understanding Marshall McLuhan." *Explorations 14, August 1968* (also available at https://www.dennislewis.org/articles-other-writings/book-reviews/marshal-mcluhan).

Lewis, Paul. 2017. "'Our Minds Can Be Hijacked': The Tech Insiders Who Fear a Smartphone Dystopia." Manchester Guardian, October 6, 2017.

Lozano, Dhariana. 2018. "6 Ways to Help Build Stronger Connection with Your Digital Communities." (https://www.socialmediatoday.com/news/6-ways-to-help-build-stronger-connection-with-your-digital-communities/533043/, accessed October 1, 2018).

McLuhan, Marshall. 1964. *Understanding Media: Extensions of Man*. New York: McGraw Hill. (The page references in the text are for the McGraw Hill paperback second edition. Readers should be aware that the pagination in other editions is different.)

McLuhan, Marshall. 1969. Counterblast. New York: Harcourt, Brace and World. https://mcluhangalaxy.wordpress.com, accessed January 25, 2021.

McLuhan, Marshall with Powers, Bruce R. 1989. *The Global Village: Transformations in World Life and Media*. Oxford: Oxford University Press.

Molinaro, M. C. McLuhan, and Toye W. 1987. *Letters of Marshall McLuhan*. Toronto: Oxford University Press.

Moreno, Megan A. 2014. "Cyberbullying." *JAMA Pediatr.* 168(5): 500.

Ortutay, Barbara. 2018. "Teens Say Social Media Makes Them Less Lonely and More Confident, Poll Finds." (http://time.com/5392314/teenagers-social-media-poll, accessed September 23, 2020).

CHAPTER SEVEN

Facebook, LinkedIn and Similar Social Media Sites

LOM: Facebook

Enhances: social interactions online; self-esteem; connectivity beyond geographic boundaries;
Obsolesces: face-to-face interactions; selectivity in making friends; physical photograph albums; privacy;
Retrieves: lost connections; village life; a sense of community.
Reverses or flips into: fake identities; fake friendships; loss of meaningful relationships; misperceptions of others; loss of privacy; keeping up appearance; online stalking; cyber-bullying; misuse of information that compromises democratic elections; government surveillance; targeted advertising based on personal user data; browsing addiction.

Facebook or Fakebook?

We start our study of individual social media sites with Facebook (FB) because it is the social medium with the most users: 2.7 billion and counting. The only online app that rivals FB in terms of the number of users is Google. The Facebook nation has a population that is more than one and a half times China's population of 1.4 Billion people. Being the social media platform that has the largest number of active users in the world, Facebook and its various technical features set the standards for interactive social media platforms and their addiction-inducing designs. Social media sites that gained popularity years after Facebook captured and dominated the social media market—such as Instagram, Twitter, Tumblr, to mention a few—achieved their user count for various reasons, some of which were luck, their specialized features like microblogging or video content and their appeal to a specialized audience based on religion, ethnicity, or sexual orientation. Those that succeeded did so in part by incorporating Facebook-like features into their apps.

All popular social media started with a relatively simple design, but their initial features and services gradually expanded over time. Facebook 2004, Facebook 2007, and Facebook 2017 have some of the same basic features, but because each new version of FB added new features they are arguably completely different platforms. Facebook has become the widest multi-media social networking site known to date as a result of the almost unlimited services and features that the platform offers. In terms of multimedia, Facebook's operating system and its digital capacity to host videos, gifs, pictures, texts, games, emojis, news links, advertisements, external links, internal links, and other minor features contribute to the complexity of the platform and allow it to hold its value as a multi-purpose communication outlet. Facebook can provide the services and features that are useful to anyone with any purpose related to online media. Users of digital technology, which form a large portion of the modern world, are bound to find at least one Facebook service that benefits them in addition to many others.

Facebook's Dominance and Popularity

Facebook founded in 2004 was far from being the first popular social networking site. It was preceded by Friendster founded in 2002 and MySpace founded in 2003. It became more popular than the others because of its constant incorporation of new features that its users found compelling. As is the case with many other commercial successes, people don't realize that they want or need something until it is given to them. Because each new feature that Facebook developed provided their users with social capital, i.e., being cool, the Facebook users were eager to try and deploy each new feature that came down the pike. Each new feature was easily incorporated into the modus operandi of each Facebook user and contributed to their social media prestige. The dynamic of user engagement and the application of each new update created a cycle of social media addiction and ongoing dependency as one feeds the other and keeps the process continuous and on-going.

Updates and new features on social media platforms are what keep users interested and active. Previously created platforms such as MySpace and Friendster failed after being relatively popular for a set period of time because 'updated versions' were not a common practice when these 'First Generation' platforms emerged. Facebook consisted of more than a few strokes of genius that allowed it to become more addictive, dynamic and interest-provoking. The year 2007 was a big win for Facebook, as the "like" feature was born and made the website wildly successful. After being active for three years, the new, simple 'like' feature that dramatically changed the way users communicate on the platform made Facebook a new, refreshed version of its old self. Facebook basically became a whole new land of opportunity for discourse, online engagement, and the construction of one's online identity. Giving and receiving social affirmation via 'likes' increased user engagement and gave people a fleeting moment of pleasure that recurs every time 'likes' were received, given, or involved in any way during online interactivity. It makes the site interactive in both directions, i.e. the sending and receiving of 'likes'.

The 'poke' is yet another feature that functions as an intermediary tool to spark possible conversation between two users. One user can 'poke' another to let them know they're interested in talking to them or simply remind them that they're using Facebook too. It's kind of a "let's connect!" hint. Poking someone in real life is a way to get their attention and the 'poke' button functions in a similar manner online. 'Share' is another Facebook feature that facilitates the transfer and distribution of information, pictures, articles, and any other posts that the platform hosts. 'Sharing' is a call-to-action that users engage with and become active participants in the circulation of Facebook posts. 'Liking' and 'sharing' are the two main user activities on Facebook and both contribute to the popularity of a post. 'Liking', however, is unique because of its more desirable connotation that alludes to validation and admiration from other users—a reaction that users find euphoric and evokes their happiness as a 'liked' individual.

The 'like' feature was so successful, that other social media platforms such as Twitter and Instagram adopted it and it became an essential part of online communication on these platforms and a necessary feature of all social media apps. A simple click that indicated whether you agreed with another user, or whether other users agreed with you, created an invisible relationship between all users on social media platforms. The idea that 'This person always likes my posts and pictures, so I obviously like theirs as well became a vital online etiquette that users abided by because they got small hits of pleasure from it. Similar trains of thought would be 'I agree with this political standpoint so I'm going to like this post' or 'I endorse this post and the user that posted it'.

Facebook is a social media platform that digitizes multiple aspects of non-digital real-life, especially social settings and multiple relationships. Facebook has even more 'friend' features than the original Friendster that pre-dated FB. It brought new meaning to the word 'friends' as friendship has become defined by simple on-line interactions as opposed to a complex face-to-face connection. Facebook's 'like' feature, comment sections, and public posting brings up this question: what effect does the medium have on content, communication, and understanding?

Facebook friendships are not limited to real-life friendships, i.e. people who have met face-to-face. Part of Facebook's popularity and booming success was the fact that it digitized all kinds of relationships, i.e. friendships, family links, social clubs, newspapers, political parties, or any collective that had a social dimension to it. By doing so, Facebook undoubtedly promoted more communication which increased its bottom line by creating more opportunities for advertising. The longer a user was online with FB the more ad revenue that was generated. Facebook created the conditions or the medium for users to easily reach one another; real life encounters, on the other hand, are much more difficult to manage for the most part. But are they only difficult relatively speaking? Is real life communication still more 'real' than online connections? Facebook 'likes', 'shares', and 'pokes' are a form of non-verbal communication that the platform makes possible. 'Likes' and 'shares' hold little meaning in our real world of face-to-face interactions but mean everything in our online lives. Are 'likes' and 'shares' forms of real communication? Or are they just tools for fake connection? Facebook initially began as a great way to communicate with estranged friends, long-distance family, and potential new acquaintances. Over time, FB introduced features such as 'likes', 'shares', and other inter-reactionary elements that altered the mode of communication online. This differs from face-to-face communication to the extent that users begin to have two distinct identities: Digital on FB and analogue in off-line real life. The online domain began as an extension of analogue communication but developed into its own autonomous on-line world. Users of FB and other social media in-habit two distinct worlds and two distinct realities, real life and virtual life, whose connections are often somewhat tenuous.

Regarding work and school life, which are considered 'formal' settings in the real world, Facebook has altered the relationships individuals have with their workplace and/or their school. Browsing work places and schools for social opportunities online is a more casual and less threatening mode of networking as opposed to the necessity of being physically present in order to network with people and represent one's self face-to-face.

Social media platforms provide users with networking tools that facilitate more than just social interactions. They also can be used for job applications, expand employment opportunities and options, and expose the user to opportunities in fields they may not have considered before. The site offers public group pages where job postings are listed with a direct inbox in which inquiries can be made and résumés can be submitted. In short, real-world processes are sped up through digital means, and individuals can perform these tasks from the comfort of their own home without, for example, needing to put on a suit and tie or a chic office outfit.

Facebook is also a communications platform that has given companies the opportunity to connect with potential employees, clients, customers with a form of advertising that does not feel like advertising and hence is more effective.

LinkedIn

Over the last decade, an application called LinkedIn has spiked in popularity and dominated the professional, business and academic networking sphere. It is not a competitor to Facebook as it appeals to a different class of potential users. In fact, there are many that use both services, FB for social life and LinkedIn for professional life. LinkedIn is the go-to professional networking platform for job searches and career building, as it provides more focused facilities than Facebook does in terms of connecting with professionals. Facebook covers a lot of ground, but a downside is that it does not specifically focus on professional networking—it's a more casual social environment than a formal career search medium. LinkedIn's focus on one aspect of online social life—professional networking—allows it to specialize in the field and as a result it has become the dominant player in the professional networking space.

LinkedIn's specialized features make the platform extremely productive by providing users with highly desirable results. Facebook can only cover so much ground as its target audience is the general public and the fact that it hosts a large array of services and information beyond a focus on professional careers. LinkedIn is a career-specific platform that provides a more focused service by connecting users directly to recruiters and human resource professionals. Facebook simply provides the opportunity to represent yourself as a possible employee along with other personal information unrelated to career specifics. LinkedIn has exclusive features such as endorsements, testimonials, and an easy-to-use online resume editor. Facebook users' home feed is flooded with different topics of interest, only some being related to employment networking.

LinkedIn home feeds are exclusively catered towards users' employment interests, career opportunities, business blogs, company news, research news, opportunities for collaborating and other professional information. If someone searches your name on Facebook, they see several aspects of your life, while looking you up on LinkedIn only gives searchers your professional profile, resume, and relevant employee skills without the personal stuff. LinkedIn is a lens through which users are seen as their professional selves only. This is not to say that Facebook does not provide several career-related facilities. LinkedIn is simply a more specialized platform, but one that bears various similarities to Facebook regarding the opportunities it gives users to explore their interests and to promote themselves.

The Education Dimension of Facebook and LinkedIn

Education is another social arena facilitated through Facebook and LinkedIn, as these platforms provide countless articles, seminars, and course materials that are available at the click of a button. Even if the educational information is not available in full form in some cases, they still provide countless links to outside sources that users can also explore with the click of a button. The advantage of digital technology is its lack of boundaries, as long as users are willing to actively search for what they seek and what they wish to be informed about. Links are the only real necessity when it comes to the spread of information in the online/Internet Age. The content does not have to be posted in full on the actual website. Facebook has the ability to be both the middle-man and the direct primary source provider. These features also pertain to LinkedIn, as it connects the user to what they seek—employment, networking, and contacts. Facebook is the middle-man in every field: education, politics, arts, career, culture, global development, friendship, travel, and virtually anything else a user could think of. LinkedIn provides a similar service for its professional users.

Facebook Filtering and Trending

Phenomena such as politics, music, and social clubs are presented on Facebook and other digital media platforms in a filtered manner. Facebook picks what to provide to users based on their previous interests and browsing history as significant topics they might be interested to explore and presents them on the platform in a more accessible manner than other subjects in general. A famous music artist could be made even more famous because they are trending online. The same could be applied to a controversial visual artist such as Banksy, a social media influencer such as Kylie Jenner, a football player like Cristiano Ronaldo, and countless others. Topics and links full of information that are available to the public are almost always the most important and influential articles on a particular subject or phenomenon.

The choices that Facebook provides its users searching for information on a certain topic is like the results of Google Search Engine search that are displayed in page and rank form. When an Internet user searches for something—a keyword, phrase, service or anything—on Google, they tend to click on the first few results that pop up which are selected for them according to popularity and functionality. In fact, 90% of adult Internet users do not go past the first page of Google results. Why would they? People want their information quickly and easily. Google provides the public with the most pertinent items of whatever topic they are searching for with 10 engaging links on only one of over 10,000 search result pages. Information overload is both a curse and a blessing, seeing as an almost endless amount of information is embedded in short links that are part of the larger data Internet-based network. McLuhan observed that electrically configured information leads to information overload and this is even more the case with computer-based digitally configured information. He observed, "one of the effects of living with electric information is that we live habitually in a state of information overload. There's always more than you can cope with (McLuhan 1967)" He also suggested that, "faced with information overload, we have no alternative but pattern-recognition (ibid.)." The pattern recognition that McLuhan suggests is so necessary is organized for us by Google's digital platform algorithms that filter out unfamiliar search results according to the user's personal browsing history.

Technically speaking, users that engage in online networking hold the ability to search anything, anywhere, at any time on the Internet. Whether they are aware of this search freedom is another story. Social networking sites like Facebook with news sections, for example, like Google, provide users with around 10 links to different news reports and blasts. Obviously, there are more than 10 news topics per day, but what Facebook and other social media websites provide directly onto individual users' personal platform feeds are stories with a slant similar to their previous news item searches. For access to any other news stories, users have to manually search or click the "view more" link on the bottom of the news section. This seems like a simple task that Facebook facilitates by providing the links, but when it comes to actual practice, users are more likely to stick to what is directly available to them on the platforms they most often use.

What Facebook renders as "trending topics" is supposedly based on what users search for most often. They are not necessarily the "trending topics" for the general population. But by making these topics a priority and categorizing them as the top stories with the easiest, most direct accessibility tends to reinforce the views of the user and shields them from alternative viewpoints.

'Trending' in which certain articles gain more search results, link clicks, and online engagements are a canonical feature of Facebook and other social media sites. The links to articles and hashtags pertaining to specific topics are said to be 'trending' when they are being clicked on and viewed by a particularly large number of users for a certain period of time. For example, trending topics on Facebook during 2016 were 'US Presidential Election', 'Trump vs. Hillary', and other subtopics related to the election such as 'Trump Facing Backlash Over Wall'.

'Trending' is a remarkable label that automatically puts a big stamp of significance on a targeted pop-culture subject, individual or global topic. The whole process of making these topics headline news turns into a full circle of the "most important topics" maintaining their title as such, simply because users are told that they are the "most important topics" and keep them trending by feeding them 'likes', 'shares', and views. They hold the most easily accessible links provided to users right on their homepage in direct view as soon as the user logs in. Is there room for anything else that Facebook seemingly decides is not important enough to trend? Global warming, for example, only recently became an important topic of conversation. Previously, people disregarded it as something unimportant in the now, and so did social media. Thus, it wasn't a trending topic and people weren't paying attention to it. The only information users have easy access to is determined by algorithms that are calculated by the social networking site ignoring what's trending in the news in general.

Politics and activism in the digital realm are shaped by this filtering process that Facebook and other social networking sites use creating a social media news canon. The algorithms used by these sites determine two main criteria that produce the chosen elements for the canon. The first is the user's personal browsing history, i.e. the websites and social media platforms most often visited in order to provide users with content similar to what they have previously searched for and engaged in. The reason that Facebook bothers to provide this service is that it enhances its bottom line. By catering to the interest of its users they increase the time that those users will stay on their site. The second criteria is "trending topics" that are determined on a less personal basis and generalized according to mass search inputs, because the trending topics will likely be of interest to their users because of their general popularity.

A combination of these two data sets, personal preferences and "trending topics" determines the direct links users are provided with which maximizes the likelihood that they will stick around on Facebook racking up more time spent on ads. Facebook stores away all other information on Google or under the "other" tab which requires an extra step that most users do not seem to have the time to take. Constant exposure to and consumption of information leaves individuals wanting a summary version of everything that is available to them and users, by and large, trust Facebook to render what's important for them to read and, more importantly, what they'd like to read.

But the question arises, does what we are interested in ever change? Shouldn't we read perspectives and concepts outside our usual reading fare? How do we step outside the box when the convenient links and suggested searches keep providing the same old stuff? When users read political news, they tend to resort to channels and media with the political views they lean towards themselves. On a general level, conservatives absorb news from conservative channels, liberals from liberal channels, and so on. The more conservatives (or liberals) click on conservative (or liberal) links respectively, the more they reinforce their views and the longer they remain on Facebook.

The difference between digital and analogue politics is that in the real world, individuals experience face-to-face communication with people holding diverse political views. There is little possibility that every conversation you have will contain information that coincides with your set views. People have arguments, discussions, compromises, and alter their opinion as a reaction to the different way they perceive the information they are exposed to. Online, the user's comfort zone is preserved as much as it possibly can be. Although other people with different political views exist, communicate, and engage online, what dominates the kind of information users get is that which reinforces their views. The news links selected to coincide almost perfectly with their viewpoint are provided over and over again, leaving the user no other viewpoints to consider and boxing them into one large uniform pool of information. It's a large pool of information that only seems unlimited, when in reality it is a small drop in the larger network of endless information. On social networking sites, users don't have to engage with opposing views but in the real world they are exposed to a greater variety of viewpoints on TV and radio and in print. The same happens with music and social clubs. Online, your suggested and predetermined taste in social conversations, engagements, and music preference confines you to a limited number of Facebook groups, music playlists, and political news provided at your convenience. Users stay stuck in the same preference because of browsing history that may have initially reflected preference but leaves no room for growth or possible changes of viewpoints.

China's Facebook-Like Social Media

Facebook is the dominant social medium in most of the world. Yet China is one of the few societies that sets itself apart from Western online platforms by constructing its own social media sites. "Weibo", launched in 2009, means "micro-blogging" and was one of the first major outlets for Chinese people to express opinions and engage with each other online. Weibo's stream of posts and information is highly surveilled as content control was deemed necessary by Chinese authorities in order to avoid social unrest. Weibo has a 140-character limit to each "weibo" or post. The platform has several similarities to Western social media such as followers, likes, shares, and graphic uploads. Sina Weibo is a more personal cyber arena as opposed to a political one seeing as posts are monitored by the government and free speech is a sensitive topic in Chinese society. However, on-line discussions on corruption and other social issues do still exist on the plat-form, despite censorship. The online environment may not be as free as that of Facebook, but online control and government intervention does not completely reduce Weibo as an un-politicized space. Facebook and Weibo hold a significant similarity regarding user-corporation/government dynamic. Weibo's flaws include hard limits to content and an emphasis on social control. Facebook's image may be that of free speech and freedom of information, but as discussed, also creates an underlying tacit social control of its own.

Conclusion

Facebook is one of the many mainstream social media that confines our interests and the information we are provided, limiting it to what we've always accepted and keeping us from the vast unexplored. If we were equally provided with all the actual information that exists, without only one favored aspect being catered to us, we would all be different people today. We all tend to categorize ourselves under similar opinions on what's interesting and what's not. It's like we're all being forced into picking a side. Democrat or Republican? Liberal or Conservative? Christian, Muslim or Atheist? Is there nothing in between? Are these the only labels we can identify with? What's more important; picking a side or understanding both sides properly? Is it possible that FB and other social media sites have contribute to the increased division and polarization between Conservatives and Liberals, Democrats and Republicans, left and right wingers? We believe that in fact social media are contributing to today's increased polarization when compared to that of the pre-social media era.

All users would have a larger diversity of interests and informed opinions if we were not so unconsciously limited. It's safe to say that the majority of social media users have become blind sheep under the illusion that what they like, read, listen to, and watch is entirely in their hands and under their control. Facebook was the first online social medium to really impact us this way, with all our browsing information and online persona details there for the taking. If Facebook's various data leakage controversies over the years have taught us anything, it's that we have reached a point where a tool—social media—has taken control of us instead of the other way around. Facebook was just the start of it and has become less popular over time with the boom of Instagram, Twitter and other popular platforms. These platforms have grown even stronger in controlling our personas and continue to do so as we unconsciously allow them to.

Reference

McLuhan, Marshall. 1967. A Remark Made During a Radio Interview on the Cbc Show: The Best of Ideas (https://torontolife.com/city/marshall-mcluhan-profile/, accessed on May 12, 2018.)

CHAPTER EIGHT

Instagram

LOM: Instagram

Enhances: sharing photos and videos; vanity; self-esteem; visual representation; taking photos and creating videos; online social interactions; flirting;
Obsolesces: text; physical photographs;
Retrieves: Narcissus; past experiences and adventures; the photo album;
Reverses or flips into: imagery versus substance; opportunity for notoriety; beauty competition; envy.

Introduction

Since 2010, Instagram has rapidly become an extremely influential social medium, altering the lives, identities, and self-perceptions of its many users. Instagram is a visual-based app on which users share photos and videos that represent their persona in digital form and allow them to engage with followers and other users through likes, comments, shares, and posts. Similar to other social media, the use of Instagram plays a big part in the way its users perceive the world and themselves.

Browsing through Instagram is a habit that a large majority of individuals participate in on a regular basis. When engaging in this easy, fast-paced browsing process, multiple things are occurring that the users are either unconscious of or choose to ignore. While looking at other people's posts and choosing whether to like, comment, or abstain, users are constantly absorbing information about how others have been living their lives, how they look, what their style is, and what they want to share with others as a representation of themselves.

Whether directly aware of it or not, Instagram users are constantly collecting information on others and their identities which they eventually use to construct their own identity. Whether we reject parts of other peoples' personalities or idealize them, what we perceive through Instagram is, to a certain extent, what we use to define and shape our own image of ourselves. Leon Festinger's (1954) social comparison theory emphasizes that individuals have a strong tendency to create self-evaluations by comparing themselves with others. The theory explains how individuals compare themselves to others in order to assess their own traits and abilities so as to define themselves according to what others would positively respond to (Dion 2016). Instagram expedites this process by being an arena in which our self-image and the images of others are constantly exposed and ready to be used as the criteria for imaging and therefore creating the ideal self.

Beverly Daniel Tatum (2000), in her work on the complexity of identity, explains how identity formation employs a process of simultaneous reflection and observation. Using Instagram provokes individuals to constantly engage in this process as they observe what other users post and compare the selectively publicized identity traits of others with their own self-image. What users post subsequently from then on tends to reflect that comparison as they insert their favourable perceptions of others into their own identity both online and offline. Individuals judge themselves in the light of what they perceive to be the way in which others are judged favourably (Tatum 2000). Instagram's version of this typology includes physical, emotional, and mental ideals related to beauty standards, financial success, intelligence, and an endless array of other features that intertwine to form one's sense of self. Each individual possesses different versions of these ideals that may or may not fit into the normative definition of achievement, happiness, and beauty. By seeing others successfully fit into the dominant ideology, those who do not belong to that group may begin to view themselves simply as substandard subordinates that are "not good enough".

Thanks to Instagram, celebrities have ceased to be anonymous figures as their personal lives are widely publicized in the media both online and offline in magazines and newspapers. The grouping of celebrity images with peer images presented on the very same platform may result in users viewing celebrities in the same light regardless of the imbalance of the social powers between them (Brown & Tiggemann 2016). Seeing celebrities' lives as a desired goal, individuals that have a keen interest in the life of a certain celebrity and a level of attraction and re-spect for them are influenced by their lifestyle endorsements of products and serv-ices (Djafarova & Rushworth 2017). Celebrities hold social and economic capital that allows them to be idolized because of their popularity, beauty and success. These celebrities construct their idealized image through their Instagram posts and share a constructed fake narrative that many people envy.

In their study on the relationship between narcissism, self-esteem, and the use of Instagram, Paramboukis, Skues, and Wise (2016) state:

> It may be that the expression of narcissistic behaviour through social networking sites is more of a by-product of a society that is becoming increasingly more "self-centred", and social media merely provide another arena in which narcissistic tendencies can be displayed. Alternatively, social media may facilitate, encourage and applaud narcissistic behaviours in a problematic spiral that magnifies the degree of narcissism even further.

Kim Kardashian and her celebrity family are a primary example of narcis-sism and unattainable idealistic standards on Instagram. The Kardashians have personified an idealistic image of financial success and beauty through the con-struction of "perfect" lifestyles that imply happiness. Being favored by social media pop-culture, what they delineate with Instagram posts that portray their lifestyle has determined and perpetuated society's normative view of happiness and suc-cess. Because of the Kardashian's ultimate lifestyle, Instagram users tend to strive towards these standards by equating content with money and Kardashian inspired physical beauty. The attributes involved in this idea of beauty can rarely be achieved naturally. The Kardashians have the upper hand financially, which a majority of Instagram users don't have, and therefore they have exclusive access to the most ex-pensive plastic surgeons, endless clothing brand options, and best beauty products including skincare, make-up, hair care, and more.

The Kardashians and other celebrities also endorse expensive products that users begin to consider a necessity for beauty. With their seemingly flawless image, these celebrities redefine what is needed to be considered beautiful and literally sell their idea of beauty by encompassing it in their Instagram posts.

The portion of non-Kardashian Instagram users who are financially able per-petuate the Kardashian ideals of beauty by mirroring the Kardashian lifestyle trends of fashions, body alterations and makeup. An integral part of confirming their achievements is posting them on Instagram for others to see and associate with their identity. Other users who are less financially capable vary in their as-sociation with these ideals and may consider themselves "lesser versions" of what they perceive to be the standards for beauty and happiness. The feedback that conformers to Kardashian ideals of beauty, fashion and lifestyle get is positive, as indicated by the "likes" and the other more explicit favorable comments they receive. The Instagram users who are less able to conform to these artificial standards of pop-culture beauty tend to feel discouraged and disappointed with themselves and are considered as deviants by others. Such unattainable standards also apply to various aspects of interest other than beauty such as music, education, humour and more. What's considered "cool" is set by the Instagram posters who have the biggest following, and that following is dependent on how "cool" these users' images remain. It's a cycle that feeds itself, constantly maintained by the fact that deviating from the online norm is a risk the majority of users would not take, as it may lead to social isolation and deterioration of self-esteem.

"Likes" and followers are the units of measurement that place users on the spectrum of online social status admirability. The more followers a user has, the higher the influential power they hold regarding the perpetuation of unrealistic ideals. "Likes" are indicative of positive feedback, and users who post images reflective of these normative standards are those who obtain the most "likes". A lack of "likes", however, indicates social rejection and a deviance of some sorts. When users don't get as many "likes" as they usually do, or are less "liked" than other users, then their self-esteem and their feeling of belonging takes a major hit. "Likes" and followers are directly associated with who is idealized, who is rejected, and who is striving towards being part of the "cool club". The issue with such a system is that users will give up their authentic identity and interests to construct a perfect but artificial image of themselves that will get them those "likes" that boost their self-esteem. "Likes" and followers have become, on a general level, a necessity for our contemporary idea of popularity and social success.

Flickr

One of the first major social media sites for the exchange of images and videos was Flickr founded in Vancouver British Columbia in 2004 six years before Instagram. At its high point it had 87 million registered users or photographers uploading images. That number has now dropped to a very respectable number of 75 million photographers who have posted half a billion images. The number of requests for images is more than 7 billion per month. (https://expandedramblings.com/index.php/flickr-stats/, accessed March 12, 2020). Flickr lost out to Instagram with only 100 million active users versus 1 billion active users for Instagram. The reason for this is it did not keep up with Instagram in terms of Facebook-like social media features. Flickr's strength, however, is "as a hosting platform for professional photographers and bloggers. Instagram, on the other hand, is strictly a social media platform for sharing photos and videos (https://www.investopedia.com/articles/markets/082015/why-instagram-winning-over-flickr.asp/, accessed March 25, 2020)."

500PX

Founded in 2009 in Toronto Ontario, 500PX caters to serious photographers providing them with a platform to display their photographs, get feedback from other photographers and perhaps finds a market for their photos through licensing arrangements. They are small in comparison to the other photo and video sharing sites with only 15 million active users but they serve an important niche for serious/professional photographers.

References

Beverly Daniel Tatum. 2000. "The Complexity of Identity: Who am I." In Readings for Diversity and Social Justice, edited by M. Adams, W. J. Blumenfeld, R. Castañeda, H. W. Hackman, M. L. Peters, and X. Zúñiga, 9–14. Abington, UK: Routledge.

Brown, Zoe, and Marika Tiggemann. 2016. "Attractive Celebrity and Peer Images on Instagram: Effect on Women's Mood and Body Image." *Journal of Body Image* 19: 37–43.

Dion, Nicole. 2016. *The Effect of Instagram on Self-Esteem and Life Satisfaction.* Salem MA: Salem State University (available online at https://pdfs.semanticscholar.org/5b94/ce76bd38768e5d406faca4c16ae34ab5dd49.pdf?_ga=2.243520323.717938788.1593643932-820867335.1593643932, accessed July 1, 2020).

Djafarova, Elmira, and Chloe Rushworth. 2017. "Exploring the Credibility of Online Celebrities' Instagram Profiles in Influencing the Purchase Decisions of Young Female Users." *Computers in Human Behavior* 68: 1–7.

Festinger, Leon. 1954. "A Theory of Social Comparison Processes." *Human Relations* 71: 17–140.

Paramboukis, Olga, Jason Skues, and Lisa Wise. 2016. "An Exploratory Study of the Relationships between Narcissism, Self-Esteem and Instagram Use." *Social Networking* 5 (2): 89–92.

CHAPTER NINE

Snapchat

LOM Snapchat

Enhances: visual dimension of online conversations; shock value; self-esteem; opportunities for humor; rapid communication; selfie culture; flirting;
Obsolesces: a record of the communication; video chats;
Retrieves: flashing; practical jokes;
Reverses or flips into: sexting; vapid interactions; vulgarity.

Snapchat is a smartphone-based application that once it is downloaded, registered and its password is set it then accesses the user's contacts on their smartphone to automatically load friends to the app. Other friend not on the contact list of the user's phone can be added as well. According to the creators of the app, Snap, Inc., Snapchat is based on the premise that "talking with photos and videos, with our real friends, [is] more personal and more fun than texting" (https://www.snap.com/en-US/news, accessed on February 18, 2020). The way that Snapchat, a multimedia messaging app, operates is that any picture, video or message that is sent to a receiver is available to that receiver for only a short time before it become disappears or self-destructs and becomes inaccessible. Snapchat differs from Instagram which is another app premised on messaging with images by the fact that messages disappear after a short time anywhere from 1 to 10 seconds depending on the choice of the sender. The messages or snaps are accessible, however, by its creator in a password protected space known as "my eyes only," if they so choose.

Snapchat introduced other mechanisms to preserve images from disappearing. One such mechanism is a feature known as "My Story." It allows users to compile their images or snaps chronologically to create a storyline, which is accessible to a group of recipients that the users of the app designate as their friends. Other mechanisms for non-disappearing images that Snapchat introduced include the following:

- Live Stories which allows participants at a public event to share images from the event that are available to all users of Snapchat;
- Official Stories in which stories of public figures or celebrities are shared for all to see;
- Custom Stories that allows users to collaboratively create stories combining their snaps.
- Memories that allows snaps and stories to be saved into a private storage area where they can be stored, edited or published as snaps, story posts or messages.

These story-based non-disappearing presentations are extremely popular and they attract more views than those of the disappearing snaps.

Another feature of Snapchat is Discover in which a user can catch the different class of stories listed above. Discover is also used by major publishers like the Wall Street Journal and National Geographic, who share their ad-supported short-form content in Discover.

Another popular feature of Snapchat is Snap Map which allows a user to share their real-time location with all of their Snapchat contacts and to see the locations of these friends who do the same.

Another feature of Snapchat that young users of the app enjoy using is Snapstreaks which occurs when two users have exchanged snaps back and forth within a 24-hour period for three days in a row. When this happens a flame emoji emerges with a number indicating how many days in a row they have exchanged snaps. Young people appreciate this feature as an indicator of the strength of their friendship.

Snapchat is a very popular social media app with billions of videos being viewed every day. It is most popular with millennials and Gen Z and is considered their most popular social media app.

Snapchat is wildly popular, with 40% of teens ages 13–17 using the app, according to 2015 research by the Pew Research Group. Consider these stats:

- In 2018, Snapchat had an average of 188 million daily active users that generated over three billion snaps a day.
- Active Snapchatters open the app 25 times a day.
- More than 60% of active Snapchatters create new content on a daily basis.
- On average, users spend 34.5 minutes a day on Snapchat and send 34 messages a day (https://www.verywellfamily.com/what-is-snapchat-and-its-use-1270338, accessed February 28, 2020).

The nature of Snapchat messaging tends to be more intimate than is the case with other social media apps like Facebook or Instagram possibly because of the self-deleting aspect of the app. The senders of snaps tend to reveal more personal aspects of their life because they know that what they send to a friend cannot be passed on to others because of the self-deleting feature of the app. Snapchat also allows them to select exactly to what friends they send intimate details of their life unlike the situation with Facebook where all of one's friend can see one's posts.

The practice of sexting, the sending of sexually explicit material, is quite rampant on Snapchat because the sender believes that the image will self-destruct in 1–10 seconds. But there have been many instances when these images have been captured and transmitted to others.

In addition to being an app for the communication among friends, a number of businesses have discovered how Snapchat can be used as a marketing tool.

CHAPTER TEN

Reddit

LOM: Reddit

Enhances: Interpretation and discussion of the news;
Obsolesces: Letters to the editor;
Retrieves: Community, newspaper and online articles;
Reverses or flips into: The Front Page of the Internet.

Reddit is not the first app that comes to mind when people think about social media like Facebook or Instagram but in fact the followers of Reddit attracts more visitors than all the other social media sites except Facebook and YouTube. It ranks number 18 in the world, number 6 in the USA and number 5 in Canada according to www.alexa.com both of which were accessed on March 1, 2020. It is arguably one of the most interesting social media sites because of the way it creates communities of interest based on stories that appear in the news or online.

> Reddit, whose astronomical popularity seems at odds with the fact that many Americans have only vaguely heard of the site and have no real understanding of what it is. A link aggregator? A microblogging platform? A social network? To its devotees, Reddit feels proudly untamed, one of the last Internet giants to resist homogeneity. Most Reddit pages have ... a few crudely designed graphics and a tangle of text: an original post, comments on the post, responses to the comments, responses to the responses. That's pretty much it. Reddit is made up of more than a million individual

communities, or subreddits, some of which have three subscribers, some twenty mil-lion. Every subreddit is devoted to a specific kind of content, ranging from vital to trivial: r/news, r/politics, r/trees (Marantz 2018).

Reddit is a Web site whose text, photo and video content and discussions of that content is provided by its users. It has been succinctly described in the fol-lowing terms:

> Reddit was started by two people Steve Huffman and Alexis Ohanian, for the sole purpose of gathering everything interesting on the monstrous internet, organize it and present to the users all across the globe. Think of Reddit as the interactive and live Newspaper of the Internet, where you'll find everything that's going on from popular articles, posts about work, TV Shows, family, business, finance, anything and every-thing. You name it and it's there on Reddit. Reddit's slogan is '*The front page of the internet*,' which when you read or go through it, will certainly seem right. Everything on Reddit is well-organized and moderated and the company consists of only 51 employees (https://geekstarts.tech/reddit/, accessed February 28, 2020).

Here is Steve Huffman's (one of the founders) description of Reddit:

> For a while, we called ourselves the front page of the Internet. These days, I tend to say that we're a place for open and honest conversations — 'open and honest' meaning authentic, meaning messy, meaning the best and worst and realest and weirdest parts of humanity (Marantz 2018).

People of various interests sign up and engage on Reddit. It is a space for anyone interested in anything. Reddit, launched in 2005, consists of more than 138,000 subreddits where each subreddit deals with a different topic. The range of topics covered by Reddit through its subreddits is encyclopedic in scope. The most popular subreddits with the number of subscribers in the millions in parentheses are: r/announcements (48.8), r/funny (27.6), r/AskReddit (25.6), r/gaming (24.4), r/pics (23.4), r/science (22.9), r/aww [Things that make you go AWW!] (22.7), r/world news (22.7), r/movies (21.9) and r/todayilearned (21.9) (https://en.wikipedia.org/wiki/Reddit, accessed February 28, 2020). If one cannot find a discussion on something of interest to the visitor they can easily start one on the topic that interests them and they are sure to find others that share that interest which accounts for its 138 thousand subreddits and growing.

One way that Reddit differs from other social media apps is its lack of speci-ficity for user content norms as is the case with other social media apps. Instagram is generically used for image-based content. Facebook specifies specific features that govern what users can post and in what mode they engage online, but not Reddit. The order in which items appear in any particular subreddit is deter-mined by the votes of the members of that particular subreddit. Each subreddit is moderated by one or more moderators. As with other social media sites Reddit generates income from advertising. It also has a premium membership that allows users to use the site free of advertising.

Reference

Marantz, Andrew. 2018. "Reddit and the Struggle to Detoxify the Internet." *The New Yorker* (March 12, 2018).

CHAPTER ELEVEN

Tinder and Other Dating Apps

LOM: Dating Sites such as Tinder

Enhance: introductions; dating; self-esteem; flirting; social life;
Obsolesce: bar scenes; blind dates; traditional dating; and introductions by friends;
Retrieve: fix ups; casual dating;
Reverse or flip into: promiscuity; hookups; sexting; one-night stands; but occasionally long-term relationships including marriage.

A Revolutionary Dating Mechanism

Social media have totally changed the dating scene for every conceivable demographic as the following list of dating sites and the audiences they address will demonstrate. At the top of the list is Tinder, the most popular and Match the very first dating site. Other dating sites include eHarmony (which tends to be pricey); Facebook Dating (which makes use of the information on one's Facebook site); OKCupid; Ship-Dating made fun again; Coffee Meets Bagel and Hinge.

In addition to these sites, there are dating sites that focus on a specialized demographic. Here is a sample of such sites:

- Christian Mingle, that matches single Christians;
- Jdate, that matches Jewish singles;
- Muzmatch, that matches Muslim singles;
- BlackPeopleMeet, that matches black and biracial singles;
- SilverSingles, that matches singles 50 years or older;
- Grindr, the largest of its kind for the gay, bi, trans and queer communities;
- Bumble, another app for the gay, bi, trans and queer communities;
- Her, that matches lesbian, bisexual, bicurious, trans, and queer women;
- Raya, exclusively for the creative industries community;
- Tastebuds, that matches people with similar musical tastes.

Roughly half of 18- to 29-year-olds (48%) and LGB adults (55%) say they have used a dating site or app. Most regard the dating apps for short term hookups, but about 20% in each group say they have married or been in a committed relationship with someone they first met through these platforms (https://www.pewresearch.org/internet/2020/02/06/the-virtues-and-downsides-of-online-dating/?utm_source=Pew+Research+Center&utm_campaign=a9f6062028-EMAIL_CAMPAIGN_2020_03_09_04_05&utm_medium=email&utm_term=0_3e953b9b70-a9f6062028-399440297, accessed March 11, 2020).

Tinder

Tinder is the most popular dating app that has become increasingly popular since its launch in 2012. In order to use Tinder, one has to be older than 18. The user can then upload a concise profile that consists of up to six images and a 500-character bio that includes where one goes to work or school. One may choose to link to their Facebook and Instagram accounts. One also enters their discovery settings that stipulate who they would like to be exposed to on the app as possible prospects and determine who sees them and who they see. These features include city parameters, gender preference, age range, religion, social media links and more.

By February 2020, Tinder had 5.9 million subscribers; by February 2018 there were 100 million downloads of Tinder and by August of 2019 there were 2 billion views per day and 300 billion matches had been made (https://expandedramblings.com/index.php/tinder-statistics, accessed March 10, 2020).

Tinder offers the convenience of perusing possible relationship prospects—sexual, romantic, platonic or otherwise—from the comfort of the users' personal smartphone's privacy. Tinder is a digital medium that substitutes the anxiety of talking to love interests or possible sexual partners at bars, coffee shops, the workplace or at school.

The app's convenience and popularity are mainly linked to its signature swiping feature as a picture and a profile appear; Swipe Right for yes, interested and Swipe Left for no, not interested. Making the yes/no decision simple, all a user needs to do to accept or reject someone as a potential interest is drag their profile page and representative picture left or right across the screen. The magic happens when two users swipe right on each other and match. They can then move on to a conversation box in which they can communicate directly and possibly coordinate a meet up.

Female/Male Perspective

The Tinder swiping process can be quite habitual and quick. It's a simple yes/no dichotomy that makes swiping and profile views a swift and rapid experience. The majority of Tinder users are heterosexual and we have found that there is a significant difference in the way men and women use the app through an informal study we made.

The co-author (MR) and a male friend both in their 20s went on Tinder to see how their experiences would differ in terms of matches and conversations that were started. While the methodology of this mini-study was extremely informal and not really rigorous, the results revealed that the experience of male and female users of Tinder are markedly different. We found from this study and others that it is common for men to constantly swipe right on a woman's profiles without observing it thoroughly before doing so. Men tend to maximize their results by swiping right on a large number of profiles and acquiring as many mutual matches as possible. They generally avoid selectivity until the 'matched' stage, where all matched users appear on a separate page that allows the initiation of a conversation in a text box. In general, the opposite happens with female users, as they tend to be pickier with the men they choose to swipe right on. Women have a larger tendency to filter potential matches as they are more selective in swiping right on other users. They tend to be more cautious when giving someone the opportunity to converse with them, thus, they swipe right mainly on users that they see as an actual prospect from the get-go. This is a mode of thought that is opposite to the male Tinder users, who prioritize widening their hook-up/dating opportunities over selectivity and accurate consideration for a potential sexual or non-sexual partner.

In short, women tend to look more thoroughly for the right person to meet, to date or even have sex with. Many men, on the other hand, tend to care less about who the person they're engaging with is and focus on the results: a hook-up or a date. Considering the visual nature of the app, it's also arguable that men have lower standards of partner attractiveness than women. Tinder users are, essentially focussed at first on the main profile picture at a glance. Men typically render 'decent looking' as 'hot' automatically because sex is often their main goal and the partner doesn't have to be super attractive for a hook-up to take place. Women's selectivity alludes to the fact that this user demographic is more analytical and observant when using the app and selecting possible partners. They prioritize potential over immediate sexual gratification, while also having higher standards of physical attractiveness simply because the average-looking woman can attract more men than the average-looking man can attract women. The following data comes from mini-study conducted by Mira Mirawdy and a male friend where they each swiped right on 100 potential matches. They wanted to test their hypothesis that the swiping practices of males and females on Tinder are different. The data clearly shows that men and women by and large use Tinder differently as the table below indicates.

Right Swipe	Total Swipes	Total Matches	Total Conversations Started (by another user)
Attractive, modest male	100	13 or 13%	2 15.4%
Attractive, modest female	100	70 or 70%	19 27.1%

Although the two subjects engaged in the same number of swipes, the female user got 5.4 times as many matches as the male user supporting our hypothesis that female users of Tinder are more selective than male users. The male users who obtained a match were almost twice as likely to initiate a conversation compared to the female users who obtained a match.

We believe that male users of Tinder are more focused on results and, in general, take more initiative on the app when it comes to swiping right and starting conversations with matched users compared with female users.

There are various systemic and social factors that contribute to the hypothesis that men swipe right more than women on Tinder. We believe that sex is still more taboo for women than it is for men. In fact, toxic masculinity and its associated culture emphasizes the idea that men's validation, confidence, and masculinity are directly linked to the number of women they encounter sexually. Conversely, women who have multiple sexual partners are commonly labeled as "promiscuous" and/or "slutty". Sexism plays a big part in the way female users and male users engage with Tinder. So, does the app perpetuate sexist ideologies? Or does it relieve women of the label because of its private usability? It's a difficult debate because of how intrinsic sexist ideologies have become when it comes to hook-up and relationship culture.

Premium Features at a Price

Tinder provides its users with optional additional features that are cost-based, unlike the app download and profile set up which are free. If the user is willing to pay for additional features they can transcend the constraints that regular users are subjected to thereby increasing the chances of being seen by their target matches and thus increasing the likelihood of making a match. Some of these key digital extra medium features, available upon paying for a Tinder Plus or a New Tinder Gold upgrade are superlike, rewind, passport, and unlimited likes.

The original concept of Tinder was that once a profile is swiped to the left, you can't get it back; i.e. you will not see it again; it's a permanent decision. But Tinder's creators and programmers have come up with a brilliant way to make money off a free app and provide users with something they wouldn't need to pay for in real life: a second chance. One of the features reproduces a rejected user's profile among the stack of other users that the swiper who originally rejected him or her is exposed to. In other words, if you spend $9.99, you have the possibility of showing up again on my screen after I've swiped left on you. It makes a swiper reconsider your profile after having previously rejected it. In other words, a profile originally rejected will be seen more than once; a concept Tinder rejected in the past but gave into in order to monetize their free digital app.

Those who are over 30 years of age will have to pay $19.99 a month for these new features. Those under 30 can get Tinder Plus for just $9.99 a month. The features included in this in-app purchase package can be broken down as such:

Feature	Tinder Plus	Tinder Gold
Unlimited Likes	✔	✔
Rewind last swipe	✔	✔
5 super likes per day	✔	✔
1 Boost each month	✔	✔
Passport to swipe around the world	✔	✔
See who likes you	✗	✔

Because it became common place to constantly swipe right, especially by male users, Tinder implemented a cap on how many right swipes you can make per day. Paying for the extra features allows unlimited likes i.e. a much higher match percentage. All other features support the same concept and act as a tool to make users more active on the app with no limitations and increase the chance of positive results and experience through the app. Tinder really worked with the idea that sex sells and found a brilliant way to profit off of users looking for a hook-up, sex, or love.

The Swiping Algorithm

Although the dating app seems to be based on a simple yes/no phenomenon, its algorithmic basis is more complicated than it seems. Each user has an 'ELO score' which essentially ranks their skill level when engaging with the app and other users on it. It's basically a desirability score that allows the app to govern who you are exposed to as possible prospects. The Tinder score depends on how much a user swipes both left and right. Simply put, nobody likes a prude and nobody likes people who are too easy to get. There's a perfect balance somewhere within the digital dating world that parallels that of real-world analog communication.

Users who swipe right too much are exposed to other people who also swipe right too much. Although swiping right by both users increases the chance of a match, it also places them within a pool of several other people who have also matched with the original swiper and decreases the chance of being noticed, lessening the possibility of a conversation being started.

For example, two users who swipe right very often will match with others who do the same. This means more matches, but it may also mean too many matches. The original pool of countless users shrinks into a smaller pool of matches, but the latter is still quite a difficult spot to be in because it's hard to be noticed in a crowd of 1,000. It's like being at a bar specified for hookups and knowing that everyone is there for the same reason; just because you are knowingly willing to start a conversation, doesn't mean you will be picked to do so ... there are so many other 'competitors' that are in the same boat.

The same process occurs when users swipe left most of the time and are pickier with their right swipes. Your chances of a match drastically decrease because you are actively making your pool of prospects smaller. But the chances of you finding someone worthwhile to talk to is also decreased because Tinder then exposes you to users who also swipe left a lot and are just as picky as you. The motive of the app's manipulation of who you're exposed to is based on the idea that realizing you are getting less matches and having less conversations is because you are too hard to get and so are other people … so you might as well start swiping right a little more and lower your standards to increase your chance of succeeding at finding someone to talk to and meet up with. It's like the real-world analog concept of "those who are too picky end up alone, and those who are too easy end up indecisive and have shallow, unworthy relationships because their standards are too low."

Sexting

Various social media apps have become a platform for visual and verbal sexting. Sexting is a portmanteau of 'sex' and 'text' and a phenomenon that has been increasingly popular among the millennial/GenZ online community. Sexting is the exchange of sexuality explicit images, videos, or texts between one individual and the other via mobile applications. The exchange of nude images and sex talk has become part of many relationships and online conversations with potential sexual partners, making sexting a digital flirting mechanism. Tinder is a key app that allows people to engage in sexting easily and builds its platform primarily as a flirty, hook-up space. Tinder is a direct medium for sexting, and the 5 pictures that users add to their profile can also be and often are a form of public sexting. Although verbal sexting is a more direct form of the concept, visual sexting is still as important and has become even more common than text due to social media's image-based platforms.

Sexting isn't always necessarily explicit—pictures that are mildly provocative can still be categorized under sexting because they evoke a similar reaction from viewers. Instagram, being a popular visual-based medium, is an app that is unconsciously or indirectly used for sexting. People portray their best-looking selves on their Instagram profile and the way users, especially women, portray their bodies, manipulate their face shape, and post attractive versions of themselves is a modern form of sexting. Original sexting began as a one-to-one exchange of sexual images and messages. The social media age has given users more opportunities to sext both directly and indirectly to a larger number of people with a subtler version of a pornographic picture. Many of the images users now post trend according to their sexual innuendo and are basically a "sneak peek" of what it would be like to sext with the original poster. This form of sexting via seductive-ideal image representation, being less scrutinized and taboo, accompanies the way in which many users construct their online profile. Their need for validation and engagement excuses their sexting, which they simply consider a proud portrayal of their confident, attractive selves.

Catfishing

There are many who catfish on Tinder and other social media by pretending to be someone they're not. Catfishing is a type of deceptive activity where a user creates a fake social networking presence, or fraud identity on a social media account. Catfishing has become a trending occurrence on Instagram and Tinder. Some users steal the online identity of others in order to portray themselves as someone 'hot' and attract attention from other app-users they feel they never would have attracted with their own physical appearance. Face-to-face conversations are more intimidating compared with the convenience of Tinder's privacy. People catfish because making up a profile and speaking to people through the safety of their phone lessens the chances of anxiety and awkwardness which are associated with face to face interactions. People even feel comfortable enough using Tinder as a communication medium behind the face of a completely different user, simply by impersonating them online via digital images. Catfishing adds another layer of being able to hide behind a screen as a completely different person with a different name and appearance to avoid presenting their true selves out of insecurity or the desire to deceive other users.

Catfishing is also used as a casual label, not necessarily referring to someone using a fake identity. If someone looks more attractive online than they do in real life, they're labeled as a catfish in Internet pop-culture. The term holds a 'deceptive' connotation alluding to someone presenting themselves very differently from what they actually are and how they actually look.

Social Media Attachments

Tinder's popularity spiked even more so when it began to spread across other social media sites such as Twitter, Tumblr, and Facebook. Tinder accounts are linked to Facebook accounts for the sake of convenience and personal information entry, such as location and occupation, transferred from one profile to the other at the click of a button. Tinder also introduced the option to link Instagram pages to one's dating profile to allows visitors to see more multimedia that represent the user and the image of themselves that they want to show others.

Tinder Doppelgangers/Imitators

Applications similar to Tinder, such as Grindr and Bumble, emerged after Tinder's peak. Grindr is catered towards the LGBTQ+ community as a target audience while Bumble's user experience is more similar to that of Tinder's. It became a substitute app for Tinder that became popular because of its smaller community and minimal traffic; there was less spam, less ads, and less fake profiles. Although it gained popularity, Tinder still prevailed as the dominant dating app, and Bumble adopted most of Tinder's features making its value to users similar to that of Tinder. Most Tinder users stayed loyal to the app or simply used both. Grindr users have a completely different online community, as the app's audience is a specific social demographic of the gay, bi, trans and queer communities.

Tinder's Upside

The debate about whether Tinder is positively or negatively impacting millennial/ GenZ society who are the major users of Tinder is a tough topic. On the one hand, it's perpetuating shallow relationships, hook-up culture, and idealist perspectives of mainstream beauty. On the other hand, it's working for many users. Despite complaints about catfishing, bad eggs, and only once-in-a-while good finds, users continue to engage on the app and use it to their benefit. Tinder is far from the worst social medium regarding the mainstream definition of beauty and toxic idealist standards of "being hot," as its only major flaw is mimicking platforms like Instagram where sex sells. Tinder cannot be held accountable as a major platform for setting these normalized standards, regardless of its contributing power and perpetuation which is undoubtedly susceptible to criticism. Tinder is like a small-scale Instagram; dangerous, but perhaps only half as deadly.

Every social medium has both pros and cons, and although Tinder has quite a few negative effects regarding self-esteem, body image, and beauty standards, the app does provide people with the opportunity to have meaningful relationships. Tinder has many success stories and a large number of its users have ended up in a committed, healthy relationship with someone they met on the app. It all really comes down to personality traits. If you're looking for a hook-up, you'll definitely find one on Tinder. If you're looking for a relationship, it might be a little harder to find someone on Tinder because of its dominant hook-up nature, but that doesn't mean it is impossible. Even relationships that start out as a casual hook-up have ended up being more serious depending on how the individuals get along. Tinder isn't really in charge of peoples' feelings, that is the users' responsibility.

The hook-up culture on the app may be overwhelming, but Tinder is essentially a place to meet people and explore your options, what happens after is ultimately up to the individuals using the service. This is the case with all social media in general. Tinder is especially useful for people who experience social anxiety, awkwardness, or hesitance with seeing what's out there. It's hard to argue that using Tinder isn't easier that approaching someone at a bar and having to look your best when you meet someone in the moment. Pros and cons. If users are just aware of what Tinder's general perceived aura is—hook-ups, optimal beauty, and sexting—they could remove that stigma from their personal profiles by posting more authentic pictures and mentioning what they're specifically looking to get out of the app in their bios, be it a hook-up, relationship, or friendship. The user has more power than they think, they just need to avoid conforming to the stigma of being a Tinder user.

CHAPTER TWELVE

Blogs, the Blogosphere and Blogging Platforms

LOM: Blogs

Enhance: the dissemination of news, personal opinions and the sharing of personal experiences;
Obsolesce: the diary, the monopoly of mainstream media and news organizations;
Retrieve: subjectivity;
Reverses or flips into: polemics.

"As for the 'fad' called blogging, the MSM (mainstream media) certainly desires it to be a fad, but the recent successes of bloggers in the political realm suggests otherwise."—Alex Kuskis, the blogger of The McLuhan Galaxy (https://mcluhangalaxy.wordpress.com, accessed January 25, 2021).

What is a Blog?

A weblog, Web log, or simply a **blog**, is a web application, which contains periodic posts on a common webpage that disseminates news and information often of a personal nature. Such a website would typically be accessible via the Internet. The roots of blogging can be traced back to the days of bulletin board systems and then to Usenet which performed a similar function to blogs with its Unix to Unix connectivity which was used to create newsgroups.

A blog is a personal online journal. Just a way of having a conversation according to some. The number of subscribers to a blog can vary from a few dozen to several millions and everything in between. Examples of blogs that attract millions of visitors include Huffpost, TMZ, Business Insider, Mashable, Gizmodo, LifeHacker, The Verge, The Daily Beast and Tech Crunch (https://phrasee.co/10-of-the-worlds-most-successful-blogs-and-what-theyre-doing-right/, accessed March 2, 2020).

But one thing for sure is that the medium of the blog, despite the opinions of many members of the established media, is not a fad but a new Web-based medium that in the past twenty-five years since the emergence of the World Wide Web has mushroomed into somewhere between 500 and 600 million blogs out of the 1.7 billion websites in the world. It is estimated that about 77% of Internet users read blogs. Blogs not only become sources of news and personal interests and opinions but they have been taken up successfully by the marketing departments of many commercial and NGO organizations because they are such an effective ways of sharing information and they are also a source of revenue for many of the more successful ones.

Although for most cases a blog is for the most part a personal journal it does have a communal dimension because of the fact that bloggers share their thoughts and reflections and their followers respond in kind with their thoughts and comments. The sum total of all the blogs and the responses from their followers/fans create what is known as the blogosphere. The items on a blog appear in reverse chronological order and they almost always provide links (1.5 billion according to technorati.com and counting) to other pages on the Internet including news stories and the comments of other bloggers. They also invite comments from their readers, which creates a sense of community.

Although blogs are written compositions they share many of the features of oral dialogue by quoting others through hyperlinking and by publishing the comments of their readers. The blogosphere is actually broken down into smaller communities of interest where individuals with similar interests and concerns follow each other's blogs. As with listservs and Usenet newsgroups which are also populated by communities of interest, there are those that produce the blogs, those that post to the blogs of others and there are those who merely lurk and only read what is posted. Lurkers usually out-number the producers and commenters but as is often the case after lurking for a long time a number of lurkers finally can no longer resist the urge to say something and they also become commenters and in some cases bloggers themselves.

The following web sites with their automated publishing system tools have stimulated the production of blogs:

- blogger.com, now owned by Google and the 15th most popular site in the world according to Alexa.com,
- LiveJournal, the 70th most popular site in the world,
- MSN Spaces,
- AOL Journals,
- WordPress,
- Movable Type,
- blogggingnetwork.com,
- squarespace.com and
- fusionrays.com.

Google Toolbar and Flickr, the photo sharing Web site, have both installed a "blog this" button to facilitate the posting of items straight in to an individual's blog.

A measure of the popularity of blogs is the fact that America Online Inc. has bought Weblogs Inc., a publisher of 85 freelance online sites about cars, movies, parenting, travel and other subjects. It is believed that AOL made this move to increase its audience size and hence its profits from ads. At first when AOL offered free blogging privileges it said it would place ads on the blogs of non-subscribers but subscribers' blogs would be ad free. They recently changed that policy and are now placing ads on the blogs of subscribers who are annoyed by this change of policy. AOL because it needs to generate more ad revenue because of their declining subscriber base is putting themselves in conflict with some of their loyal customers and this could backfire on them.

There are guides to help readers find blogs that they might wish to read. For example there is https://www.blogarama.com/en/, which claims to be the oldest blog directory, as well as http://www.bloggernity.com; https://alltop.com; and https://blogs.botw.org to mention a few.

The Blog as a News Medium

Blogs provide an alternative news service and as a result cover items that might not appear in mainstream news outlets. They also provide a channel of communication for journalists in countries where they are not allowed to publish their stories. In Iran where media censorship is quite severe as of 2016 there were 2 million blogs. Some of the bloggers were harassed by the government and actually arrested but given the large number of blogs the Iranian regime has been unable to stem the flow of authentic news and information from Iranian bloggers (https://en.wikipedia.org/wiki/Media_of_Iran, accessed March 2, 2020).

In certain instances, bloggers have had more of an impact on the flow of news than the owners of small-town local newspapers ever had. So, to influence public affairs one does not need to be a media mogul and own large circulation newspapers and magazines or a television station. Rather one can learn to make effective use of a blog. If the Internet is like a "global village" as many have suggested, then blogs are its village newspapers or town criers.

Some have argued that bloggers are not really journalists but that is not the way a California appeals court saw things in a decision it made in May 2005 when it ruled that the same confidentiality laws that apply to traditional journalists also apply to bloggers operating as journalists. They wrote, "we can think of no workable test or principle that would distinguish 'legitimate' from 'illegitimate' news … Any attempt by courts to draw such a distinction would imperil a fundamental purpose of the First Amendment (https://www.facebook.com/sjtalkshow/posts/10205018673417777, accessed Jan 31, 2021)."

Blogs as Defense against Media Concentration and Monopolies of Knowledge

Harold Innis (1951) long ago formulated the notion of monopolies of knowledge (and opinion), which at first were controlled by priests in oral societies followed by copyists in the age of handwritten manuscripts. These monopolies were then neutralized by the printing press but a new monopoly of knowledge developed by those who controlled the printing presses and later by those who controlled broadcasting outlets. The concentration of media ownership exacerbated the tendency towards the monopolization of knowledge and especially opinion. The Hearst newspaper chain of the late 19th and early 20th centuries is a notorious example.

The fears that Innis expressed in 1951 have abated somewhat because computing and connectivity, such as the Internet, that have led to open systems in which information is free to flow. Small elites are no longer as able to completely control the creation of wealth and the flow of information. The Internet and the World Wide Web have played a prominent role in the breakdown of Industrial Era monopolies of knowledge by providing a medium whereby non-professionals have been able to share their experiences and opinions and network their knowledge.

Web sites that act as electronic support groups have sprung up all over the Net providing practical suggestions for those who have to cope with a variety of different political, economic, medical, psychological and social problems. Bloggers represent a further evolution of this trend not only for political opinion but also support and information for a variety of interests and concerns.

Blog Hosting Platforms

There are a number of Web site apps that facilitate the production of a blog.

Name of the App	Websitebuilderexpert.com description	Alexa.com global ran
Wordpress.com	– powerful built-in blogging tools.	60
Tumblr	– ideal for sharing short-form, clickable content.	88
Go Daddy	– quick to set up, but lacking real quality.	168
Wix	– perfect for combining a blog with a website.	208
Blogger	– good choice for a very basic blog.	255
Weebly	– number one for building a blog quickly and easily.	307
Squarespace	– stunning blog designs and images.	456

(https://www.websitebuilderexpert.com/website-builders/best/blogging-platforms/, accessed March 2, 2020)

Podcasting, Photo Blogging and Vlogging

Podcasting is an audio blog as podcasters must use the Web and a Web site to transmit their podcasts. Two other forms of blogging have emerged making use of visual media, namely the photo blog and the video blog or vlog. As with blogs these formats give these AV bloggers the opportunity to find an audience and to hone their radio editing, photography and videography skills, respectively.

Reference

Innis, Harold. 1951. *The Bias of Communication*. Toronto: Univ. of Toronto Press.

CHAPTER THIRTEEN

YouTube

LOM: YouTube

Enhances: sharing different forms of media including videos; audios; movies; TV shows; personal narratives; and the creation of online communities;
Obsolesces: exclusivity of cinema trailers; TV broadcasts; video stores;
Retrieves: TV, movies, music, news reels and documentaries from the past;
Reverses or flips into: a collection of documentaries.

The Boundless Scope of Content

YouTube is a video-sharing website and social media platform on which users create and upload original content that they or others have created representing an endless variety of material. It is one of the most popular destinations on the Internet second only to Google.

Users of YouTube are free to both upload and view content. They are also able to rate YouTube content and indicate what their favorite content is. Users can create their own playlists and share their favorite videos with friends. The sharing of favorite videos contributes to the social media dimension of YouTube as does their ability to comment on the videos that they view.

YouTube is for the people and by the people, making it abundant in user generated content (UGC) and heavily influenced by users' feedback in the comment sections and on other social media platforms that link back to YouTube. It is the comment section that contributes to its social media dimension. Another social media dimension is the channel's feature that allows an individual or a group of individuals to create a collection of videos and audios with a uniting theme, known as a channel. A YouTube channel operates as a vlog (video blog).

Features

YouTube's platform features are similar to those of other social media—in terms of feedback, the users' main tools are likes, dislikes, comments, and subscriptions. YouTubers, i.e. those that post on YouTube, thus have a measurable understanding of how their content is performing on the platform through direct user feedback. A significant popularity metric is view count (how many times the content has been seen), which is clearly visible under the video itself and indicates how well it is received by subscribers and the general user public. This metric is highly valuable because it provides an indication of whether the content is worth engaging with. The digital space is a fast-paced environment, and users are highly influenced by what other users seem to like or dislike, so seeing a high view count on content is likely to persuade visitors to engage with it. The quality of content on YouTube is, in a sense, predetermined according to the metrics that indicate its popularity, regardless of its actual quality which can only be actually determined subjectively after users experience it.

The term, YouTubers, refers to users that create content and have accumulated a significant social following (subscribers) that keeps up with what they post. Channel Users refers to those subscribers or participants on the platform that view content. All users have a 'Recommended' section on their YouTube homepage that suggests content they would be interested in according to a search algorithm. It is at the top of each homepage and is thus the first thing users see when they enter YouTube. The recommended section of the platform plays the biggest role in guiding user behavior and navigation as they choose what to watch next. More than 70% of time spent on YouTube is spent watching what the algorithm recommends (www.hootsuite.com, accessed December 16, 2019). YouTubers increase the chances of their content showing up in the recommended section if they play by the algorithm and Google's rules. The algorithm influences both what YouTubers produce in content and what users are more likely to watch. In order to assess how the platform is used and its implications of popularity, we must look at what its algorithm prioritizes as 'quality content' which Google promotes to the public and puts more of a spotlight on. That content is what goes viral and sets trends.

The algorithm ranks search results on YouTube according to two primary factors: how well the YouTuber's content metadata (title, description, keywords) fits the searcher's query and how much the content has engaged users already. The latter is assessed by the likes, comments, and watch time that a video has. However, YouTube insists that search results are not a list of most-viewed videos for a given query (ibid). There are more factors that play a role in how many users will have clearer access to content. By clearer access, we mean that some videos pop up on the recommended list and are more likely to be clicked on by users that would have otherwise not gone through an organic search to find it them-selves. According to YouTube, specific user behaviors are part of what guides the algorithms choices. These behaviors include whether a video is watched in full or simply clicked on and then abandoned after a few seconds. The algorithm also pays attention to how quickly a video's popularity snowballs, how new the video is, how often the YouTube channel (YouTuber) uploads a video, and how many likes, shares and engagement the content is receiving. The algorithm is far from simple, but its determinants' obvious common denominators are engagement and user in-terest according to the feedback they leave. What helps improve that engagement is YouTubers' content quality and whether they are adjusting their posting strategy to what Google has established as a best practice.

Channel Typologies

YouTubers are basically vlogging (video blogging) and thereby transforming textual blogging with their audio-visual content. They are able to create on YouTube channels that become a social media platform for them as much as is the case with Facebook and Instagram. They are also able to make their channels open only to subscribers and hence create a revenue stream for them-selves. The top ten channels most subscribed to with their number of subscribers in the millions and the language of their service in parentheses are: T-Series (129, Hindi), PewDiePie (103, English), Cocomelon—Nursery Rhymes (73.8, English), Set India (65.6, Hindi), 5-minute Crafts (64.6, English), Canal Kondzilla (55.7, Portuguese), WWE (55, English), Justin Bieber (51.5, English), Zee Music Company (50.6 Hindi), and Dude Perfect (49.3 English) (https://www.brandwatch.com/blog/most-subscribed-youtubers-channels/, accessed July 2, 2020).

The gap between YouTube and the traditional business community has started to narrow given the platform's take-off as a money-making machine for many content creators and innovators. In fact, those uploading content to YouTube include in addition to individual 'YouTubers', companies and corporations that use their YouTube content to promote their goods and services.

YouTube, purchased by Google, has been its subsidiary since 2006. Each user's Google account is automatically linked to their YouTube account, whether they are content creators or simply viewers on the receiving end. YouTube is one of the most interesting social media platforms, although it did not initially start out as a traditional social website. This boundless platform is home to educational videos, personal experience stories, clips from movies, music videos, comedy skits, social reform opinions, news, news reel clips from the past and generally everything in between. Folks have uploaded vintage videos and audios from live performances in the past so that one can travel back and view things that took place before one was born. If there exists a video about it or recording of it, it's probably on YouTube.

YouTube offers a wide variety of user-generated, user curated and corporate media videos. Private individuals, unaffiliated with a predetermined brand, have used YouTube as their voice and outlet, appealing to users with content that is insightful, informative, entertaining, and, in some cases, heavily controversial. Some YouTubers make videos about cooking, others about interview tips, some make DIY tutorials, many just make entertaining videos about themselves. It's all subjective and widely diverse—people like to watch different things and creators like to create different things. Entertainment is very broad in scope, and YouTube makes searching for what interests or entertains you—or better yet, captivates you—an easy yet addictive journey.

The mechanics of the YouTube platform make it hard to stop watching video after video, especially when the average video length on YouTube is about 4 minutes and the platform has an auto-play feature that jumps from one video to the next if the user doesn't manually pause. This feature was installed to keep the visitor on the site as long as possible because the longer the user is on the site the more advertisements they will view and the more revenue they will generate for YouTube, Google's subsidiary. Why four minutes? That's what our attention span loves. Why read a 300-page mystery novel when you can watch a YouTuber tell a 4- or 5-minute story about how their crazy neighbor sabotaged their crazier brother-in-law? Why watch a 30-minute show about relationships when you can subscribe to a YouTuber that talks about her own relationship experiences, and experiences that her friends have also had. Real experiences told by real people, unfiltered relative to mainstream media that tends to push an agenda, through cultivated narratives. It's like reality TV on crack, but with less scripted narratives and more personal, relatable stories.

With YouTube, much like many other social media, you can turn from a nobody into a somebody overnight. All you need is entertaining content, good lighting, a camera, and an audience that not only wants to see what you have to offer, but also supports you via comments, likes, subscriptions, and promoting your YouTube channel on their other social media platforms and sharing your content. You can be a tech guru, a foodie, a gardening enthusiast, a stay-at-home parent, a fifty-year-old, a four-year-old (yes, there are toddlers who make more money than corporate employees), a high school dropout, a university professor, it seriously doesn't matter. Labels on YouTube become less like definitive boxes and more like life stories. If you give an audience something they're interested in and focus on quality, you can accumulate a large number of subscribers and make advertising money off of whatever it happens to be you make videos of. As we discuss YouTube further, it will become apparent that there are many ways to hold the attention of your subscriber base. The other category of users—those who watch what others create—undergo a variety of experiences thanks to the diversity of the platform. Users can live vicariously through YouTubers and learn about anything from cooking an egg to switching careers in their 40s or 50s.

Omnichannel Equity

YouTube became increasingly popular after its launch in 2005, but one of the extra boosts to the platform's popularity was triggered by the shutdown of Vine in 2016. Vine was a short-form video hosting service where users could share six-second-long looping video clips. The app became favored by many and allowed 'Viners' to create a brand for themselves, build a following, and become 'social media famous'. Vine stars like Logan Paul, Lele Pons, David Dobrik, Josh Peck, Brandon Calvillo and many more started out as ordinary teenagers, then got so famous through Vine that the app became their full-time job. Viners with a large following could make anywhere between $20,000 and $50,000 per ad campaign. Third party companies prioritized these users as 'social media influencers' and connected them to a brand that they can help sell to their followers. Vine influencers would promote a product in one of their Vines and recommend their followers buy it. Influencers made their Vines an advertisement to start making money and sustain their career. Users were somewhat aware of the fact that the ads and Viners were sponsored, but seemed to move past it because they loved the content and loved the creators. Followers loved the Viners as much as they love their celebrity crush and Vine influencers became the celebrities of the digital age.

After Vine announced it will be shutting down in 2016, Viners struggled to find a way to continue their content creation and preserve their bond with followers. YouTube was the answer. After Vine's official end in 2017, big Viners were already on YouTube with an almost equal number of followers as they had on Vine, having asked their followers to subscribe to their YouTube channel by communicating with them through other social media platforms, mainly Twitter and Instagram. And why wouldn't they? People had been using YouTube for years anyways, and subscribing to creators they already knew and loved was an easy transition.

Branding and Earning

It is of extreme importance to differentiate between YouTubers' channels and other branded channels. YouTubers are content creators that have self-branded by accumulating subscribers and gaining popularity one video after the other. They are their own brand and product. Other channels exist as a brand continuation via social media presence such as TV shows for example. Popular branded entertainment such as talk shows, reality series, and other traditionally televised content have adjusted to the YouTube takeover and established a presence on the platform to stay relevant in the eyes of the world. Since YouTube is the new TV, those who once considered TV to be the best platform for their audience have noticed the digital shift in entertainment traffic and moved their content onto YouTube. These known entertainment brands, such as The Daily Show, Dr. Phil, Family Feud, and many others post compartmentalized content and snippets of their TV-aired shows on a YouTube channel so that those users who have abandoned TV as a medium don't necessarily abandon the content itself.

Anyone who wishes to be successful on YouTube, content creator or conglomerator, needs to post consistently and continuously. Making money on YouTube by ad hosting within content also requires continuous uploads and building a loyal, regularly engaged audience. On average, a YouTube channel can receive $18 per 1,000 ad views. Usually channels place a 5 second ad—that which YouTube determines—at a point in their content that is of peak interest, so viewers are more likely to endure watching the ad in order to continue watching the content. On the other hand, many users are annoyed when too many ads are in a video when content quality is low and not worth the wait. The world of money-making on YouTube is quite the game—being 'monetized' or eligible to host ads has strict requirements that content creators need to play by while still maintaining interesting content. YouTube's monetization policies disfavor channels that post repetitious or reused content, so YouTubers are more motivated to produce innovative content. The fresher the content, the more likely it is to get a higher view count and make money in ads—YouTube takes the bulk cut and the YouTuber gets a mere fraction by being a middle man, but that fraction can quickly turn into a fortune if accumulated through loads of views. Content is clearly key, but community is king. On a platform that is built by and for users, only they ultimately determine how engaging the channel's content is. They determine not only how much YouTubers get paid, but how much YouTube itself earns as a company.

YouTubers reach a point at which they create multiple streams of income after establishing a sizeable subscriber aggregation. Sponsorships start rolling in—a brand-YouTuber business relationship develops in which content creators get paid to promote products and services to their subscribers. Sponsorships are discussed more thoroughly in a Chapter Nineteen dedicated to influencer branding, as product endorsement is a fundamental component of cross-functional social media earnings—and primarily the way by which social media has become a high earning job for some. YouTubers collaborate with brands and sell their products to subscribers, earning a commission in return for their promotion. YouTubers also commercialize their own brand by selling merchandise to subscribers. "Merch", as YouTubers and subscribers call it, not only generates income for the creator, but also plays a role in building a sense of community and belonging. Users that purchase YouTuber merch do so to support the creators they admire and become an affiliate of their brand—part of their community. That community is not only present on YouTube, it's across several social media platforms. A user that admires and subscribes to a YouTuber's channel will also likely follow them on Instagram and Twitter. YouTubers and content creators hold follower equity on multiple platforms.

YouTube versus TV

Gaining popularity over the years, YouTube has also become an archive host for media that were once exclusive to television. Since the Internet reaches a wider audience than cable TV, and is cheaper than subscribing to a media provider, the platform has come to replace television for many as an easy access, user-specific platform that provides entertainment beyond sitcoms, talk shows, and the 6 o'clock news. If you cannot fight them then join them. It is for this reason, production companies have been using YouTube to grow audiences by posting on their YouTube channel what they broadcast on TV. Corporate media YouTube channels such as CTV and CNN post excerpts of their broadcasts on the platform that function as highlights or flash briefings, reining in more viewers than they do on national television for a variety of reasons including scheduling and mobility. YouTube has another advantage in that it has suggestions in the form of quick links, whereas TV presents content as a set of channels that are not particularly catered to users' interests.

The perks of YouTube are plenty for known brand names such as BBC, Vogue, GQ, Betty Crocker, and more. Whether the corporation focusses on news, fashion, pop culture, cooking, cars, the environment, or pet care, there is always an advantage to presenting all their content on a YouTube channel. People are more likely to use their laptops rather than their TV to watch what they want to watch, whenever they want to watch it. People who aren't into hour-long documentaries about climate change now have an alternative for educating themselves. They can choose to view National Geographic's YouTube channel, or a specialized scientist's channel, or a group of environmental activists' collaborative channel. The sources, topics, and perspectives are limitless. You can look up mental health on YouTube and learn from a psychologist, a therapist, a parent whose child experiences anxiety, or just another person like yourself who struggles with mental illness and tells their tale and give hope to watchers. Whose opinion is more credible? A better question would be, whose perspective is focused on educating, and whose perspective is focused on capitalizing?

The most notable switch that we've seen from TV to YouTube occurred during the COVID-19 pandemic in 2020. Although the platform was experiencing an exponential increase in user traffic well before quarantine measures were taken, the need for physical distancing halted TV production by a significant amount, leading broadcast shows to make a full-time switch onto the YouTube platform in order to keep their businesses alive. Instead of posting only snippets of their shows on YouTube, productions like the Ellen Show, Late Night with Jimmy Fallon, and many others fully converted their TV productions into YouTube content. In a time where connecting with people became physically impossible at broadcasting studios and venues, virtual connections took the lead. YouTube has become the solution to various hinderances that TV productions face: the need for physical attendance (cast, crew, viewers in the audience), user attention span, cost of TV provider subscriptions, audience targeting … the list is endless. YouTube beats TV at the convenience game on multiple levels, which is why it only seems natural that broadcast TV productions could eventually fully migrate onto the social media platform where their viewers are most present.

CHAPTER FOURTEEN

TikTok: The New Wave of Content

LOM: TikTok

Enhances: humor;
Obsolesces: Snapchat;
Retrieves: karaoke;
Reverses or flips into: addiction.

Introduction

Being the most recently popular social media platform, TikTok is an interesting social media platform to observe from its recent birth. Some compare it to Vine, because of its short content duration (each video is 15–60 seconds long), others talk about it like it is the most unique innovation to date. Just like Facebook and Instagram were at their start, TikTok is fresh, new, and never-been-done-before. All social media are unique until they are not. At some point, everything integrates. Influencers start posting content there in addition to their other social media platforms, celebrities try to stay relevant by creating a TikTok account and dancing, and businesses start marketing by integrating ads into TikTok's For You feeds. Platforms follow similar paths in growth and evolution in the digital world.

Facebook, Instagram, YouTube, Twitter, TikTok—they're all different but fundamentally the same. Whenever a new social medium pops up, users are quick to engage, post, and attempt to become influencers. It's the new career dream in the digital age. And why shouldn't it be? It's money-generating and gives people the opportunity to pursue their passion and share it with others at the click of a button.

There are two versions of TikTok, the version that the readers of this book are familiar with and a version in China that goes by the name Douyin which was the original version launched in September of 2016 in Beijing by Bytedance, a company founded in 2012. The TikTok version, virtually identical to Douyin, was launched in the international market a year later in September 2017 and became an instant hit especially among the younger set of users. The app runs on different servers in each of the markets it serves and is available in 75 different languages. The videos that it features falls into two categories: (1) 3–15 second music videos and (2) short looping videos that run anywhere from 3 to 60 seconds.

TikTok is a video-sharing social media platform that has gained an insatiable amount of popularity since its international launch in 2017. Having first started out as a social networking service in China, it later on expanded to other countries and became the most downloaded app in both 2018 and 2019, having a whopping 800 million monthly active users. Its user count is in close competition with Facebook and Instagram, surpassing the popularity of Twitter, Snapchat, and Reddit. TikTok is the number one downloaded app of 2020 and has introduced a new wave of social media influencers, content creation, memes, and digital trends.

One of the most followed users on the app is Charlie D'Amelio, who acquired over 62 million followers. In a 2020 interview with Jimmy Fallon, Charlie claimed authenticity to be her greatest tool in social media success. Overnight, the 15 year-old turned from a nobody to a somebody by posting a video that went viral, making her a star and influencer from that point forward. Unlike other social media platforms, TikTok's unique algorithm provides content creators with a higher chance of going viral due to its novelty and relatively "celebrity-free" culture. For a little while, everyone on the app had an equal chance to be seen on the app. Although Hollywood celebrities have now joined the app in greater numbers, and Influencers from other platforms have transported their follower equity from other platforms onto TikTok, the app is still a digital space in which the everyday user has as much of a chance to be noticed as does a celebrity or an influencer on another app. After all, those influencers were nobodies before they went viral.

After its official international launch in 2017, TikTok was avoided by a large number of social media users who deemed it "weird" and "for kids". Even I (MR) personally avoided using it, not seeing the point as an outsider, until I decided to take a peak for research purposes, knowing it would be important to include in this publication. Now I'm hooked and spend hours on end scrolling through my feed, observing everyone's innovative content. In 2019 and 2020, the app became increasingly popular and is now following in the footsteps of other social media platforms like Instagram when it comes to ad hosting, digital marketing, content trends, and aesthetic standards. Currently, the algorithm is very generous and gives all users a high chance of going viral and making an appearance on the "For You" page—the content feed that TikTok users have that can be compared to YouTube's "Recommended Page". The For You page is full of user-generated content and videos that users post full of voice-overs, skits, music, and above all, dances. The app's essence is dance performance videos—songs and dances go viral on TikTok, after which various users participate in dance trends and post videos of them-selves 'doing TikToks'. Although dancing is a main component of TikTok content, the platform is a host for virtually anything users are interested in making: art, cooking, dancing, comedy sketches, advice, botany, you name it.

Social Impacts and Self-Perception

The TikTok app's usability boasts an endless stream of content, as users keep swiping upwards on their smartphone screens to browse one video after another. The process can be very addictive given that (1) videos are short in duration and users today for the most part have a short attention span and a preference for short-form content and (2) the user interface has a mechanical transition from one video to the other—swiping is addictive and it's difficult to stop once you've started. As we all know, social media is generally addictive, and browsing other people's content and posts about their lives—whether they are accurately depicted or not—helps us avoid focussing on our own lives. Social media platforms are an effective distraction from real life. Although they have various positive impacts, which are necessary to assess alongside the negatives, apps like TikTok, Instagram and Facebook can be so addictive that they totally capture users' attention and hinder beneficial social interactions.

Addiction to apps like TikTok also impact users' self-images and personal perceptions. The more time we spend looking at other people's content, the more we tend to compare ourselves to others. The way we look, behave, create content, and speak is heavily influenced by social media users who have a large follower and 'like' count. They become the ideal image of being someone worthy of admiration and attention, so users tend to shape their personality around what's trending. Some successful content creators promote authenticity and inspire watching users to be their authentic selves. Other content creators promote a more stagnant self-image, causing users to abandon their authentic persona in pursuit of one they think is more likely to gain admiration. This façade persona can be exemplified by idealized beauty standards, a specific body image, a "Western" way of speaking, and limited potential to expand beyond what is considered "acceptable" in modern society. Some users are sheep in a herd, others are solo birds in the sky—it all comes down to being aware of how our media affects us. As always, and as McLuhan emphasizes over and over, our media are an extension of ourselves, and if we are not aware of that fact, we give them the power to govern us. It's important to pick and choose how we want our media to change us, hopefully for the better. It can be inspiring to see TikTok content creators being their authentic selves and thus helping us help us to aspire to likewise be our own authentic selves also. However, it can be discouraging and making us believe we are unattractive when they exploit their sexuality or body image to attain their popularity.

CHAPTER FIFTEEN

Twitter

LOM: Twitter

Enhances: immediate online communication to multiple followers; personal narratives; public participation through the creation of the twitter-verse; commercial promotion;

Obsolesces: email, breaking news on TV; newspaper headlines; interviews;

Retrieves: the telegram and Telex; announcements; polls; PR;

Reverses or flips into: the banal; narcissism; propaganda; unsubstantiated claims; fake news.

Introduction

Twitter is a social medium in the form of a social networking service that enables users to send and read short 280-character messages called "tweets". Twitter began as an internal texting medium for a podcasting company called Odeo in 2006, which morphed into Twitter, Inc. a year later. When Twitter first went online in 2007 a tweet only contained 140 characters, but that number was increased to 280 characters in November of 2017. Registered users can read and post tweets, but unregistered users can only read them.

Twitter is used to help friends keep in touch with each other and to announce things of mutual interest to a group of friends and associates or to promote something to the general public of one's followers. Twitter is used by politicians to maintain the support of their constituents and to garner public support for policies they wish to enact. It is used by celebrities so their fans/followers can keep track of them and so they can promote their brand. Twitter is used as a medium for advertising by companies and NGOs. It has also been used to alert folks of emergencies. Twitter was the way many people first learned of the disaster associated with the bridge collapse in Minneapolis in 2007 as a result of the many tweets that propagated through local Twin-City networks.

The Top Ten Tweeters in Terms of Followers

The top 10 tweeters in terms of the number of followers are in order with the number of their followers in the millions: Barack Obama (129), Justin Bieber (114), Kate Perry (109), Rihanna (101), Cristiano Ronaldo (91), Taylor Swift (88), Lady Gaga (84), Ariana Grande (81), Ellen DeGeneres (79), and YouTube (73) (https://friendorfollow.com/twitter/most-followers/ accessed January 26, 2021). Donald Trump came in at number 7 with 83 million followers in the above ranking on July 3, 2020. But because he was banned from Twitter after his ignominious inciting of the January 6, 2021 insurrection and the attack on the U. S. capitol he now has zero followers. His use of Twitter was quite different than the use of all other users of Twitter, in that, aside from news outlets, he sent out the most tweets 53,382 as of July 3, 2020 of any other tweeter. Barack Obama, with the most followers only tweeted 15,856 times in the same time frame.

What You Say Counts

One of the most important elements of Twitter users' online experience is the platform's hierarchy of favored content, namely text-based tweets versus visual representations. Users engage on Twitter via text primarily, although images and videos were integrated into the platform format a few versions after its initial launch in 2006. Inbound and outbound content generated and received by users personify opinions, humor, interests, and other unique characteristics. What we ought to take from this recognition is that communication and personal representation on Twitter is essentially based on what you say, not on what you look like. That's a bold, generalized statement to make, as visual posts on Twitter do play an important part in the way we absorb information and communicate our thoughts. It would then be more useful to say that Twitter is one of the only popular social media platforms that allows its users the opportunity to represent themselves on-line without a spotlight on physical appeal in order to 'fit in'. In comparing user experiences on Twitter to those on Instagram, it is Instagram that uses material culture and sex appeal to gain the attention of its audience. Twitter is seemingly the opposite as a larger portion of users gain popularity and positive feedback from text-based content exclusively. On Twitter what you say counts and images merely complement the thoughts you share. This is quite different than most social media where images are paramount as is the case with Instagram, Facebook and TikTok for example.

Keeping It Short and Sweet

The need for keeping messages short in digital media favors instant messaging and Twitter and hence accounts for their success. Marshall McLuhan was one of the first to observe that with electrically configured information there is a pref-erence for shorter messages. He, himself, enjoyed using one-liners or epigrams because he believed that the one-liner was all the attention his readers would be able to muster. Although this is certainly a stretch, we would like to suggest that with his advocacy of one-liners, McLuhan foreshadowed the idea of Twitter that a short succinct message is all we have time for. He wrote: "We've invented the one-liner in place of the joke because people cannot wait around to hear you tell a joke ... That's all we have time for. Attention span gets very weak at the speed of light (McLuhan, M., S. McLuhan and Staines 2003, 271)." Twitter is nothing more than one-liners transmitted by the Internet. McLuhan's one-liners are actu-ally less than the original 140-character limit and absolutely less than today's 280 characters. "The medium is the message," for example contains only 25 characters including the spaces.

One of the critiques of Twitter has been that it promotes superficial com-munication. Tweets have been likened to newspaper headlines. The difference is, however, that the headline had a story to back up that headline with informative details. Tweets, however, are the whole story with no further elaboration of the Twitter headline.

Twitter has also been likened to sound bites. A sound bite is a short clip, usu-ally of speech, that is extracted from a longer narrative and is often times used to promote the full piece. The difference between a tweet and a sound bite is that with the tweet there is no longer narrative; the tweet is all you get.

Twitter Features

Retweeting: Tweets that are received can be reposted to one's followers with or without a comment using Twitter's retweet icon. One can also retweet one's own tweets.

Hash tags: Hash tags are a way of tagging a tweet to make it easy for followers to find it as part of a series of tweets on a particular topic. A hashtag is similar to a thread in a series of emails focussed on a particular topic. A hashtag begins with the number sign, #, as in #topic.

Photos and videos: Twitter allows the uploading and downloading of photos and videos, video streaming and even the live streaming of events.

URLs: URLs can be included within a tweet and Twitter provides a service that allows long URLs to be shortened as the URL that is posted contributes to the character count.

Twitter bombs: Twitter bombs is a form of twitter spamming in which numerous tweets with the same hashtag are made with the goal of advertising a certain idea or product.

Reference

McLuhan, Marshall, Stephanie McLuhan, and David Staines. 2003. *Understanding Me: Lectures and Interviews*. Toronto: McClelland and Stewart.

CHAPTER SIXTEEN

Pre-digital Age Monopolies

In this chapter we will explore the phenomenon of monopoly formation before the digital age so as to understand how the formation of monopolies changed with the advent of the digital technologies of personal computers, the Internet and the World Wide Web. As we will discover monopolies have been a fact of life throughout human history beginning with chiefdoms that date back to Palaeolithic times.

Before the formation of chiefdoms humans organized themselves in what scholars have deemed Big Man societies (Johnson & Earle 1987). A 'big man' is the leader for a local group consisting of many related nuclear families. He is critical for internal dispute resolution, risk management, trade and intergroup alliances. He is a charismatic leader who rules at the pleasure of his followers and can be replaced by a rival. He does not control all of the resources of the community of which he is the head nor does he take the lead in all the activities of his society leaving that to the local experts who are not necessarily related to him or beholden to him. That all changes with the evolution from Big Man societies to Chiefdoms which emerge as the population of local groups increased.

The Chiefdom is similar to the local group in terms of the economy but there is enough richness so that a surplus is generated often through capital investments such as irrigation, fishing boats, or trade. The surplus is used to support the chief's activities, which includes conquest of other local groups, which are incorporated into the polity rather than excluded as in the case of local groups. Leadership is controlled by a hereditary elite at both the local and regional level and is legitimized by ceremonies. With the death of a chief a competition begins to succeed him which results in a new regime of office holders

The intensification required to support ever increasing population densities gives rise to technologies that allow a chief to create a **monopoly** and control the centralized economy of the polity. The chief owns the wealth, which is redistributed and also serves as a form of risk management. The redistribution of wealth also provides a way for the chief to finance the various activities that he carries out, which includes the co-ordination of trade, the management of the production economy, the mediation of disputes, the conduct of defence and warfare. The society stratifies into a ruling elite and commoners. The chief is assisted by other members of his elite cohort. Ceremonies are used to legitimize his power (Logan 2007, 282–83; our bolding).

With the Neolithic Revolution circa 10,000 years ago the cultivation of plants and the domestication of animals gave rise to a significant increase in the population of local groups and the size of territory occupied by them. As populations increase there was a transition from chiefdoms to states and with it an increase of the power and scope of monopolies. Those that owned the land and controlled it had a monopoly of this resource that is vital to food production. The local residents of the land became serfs whose existence depends on the land-owning aristocracy. In addition to the access to the land there is also the dependence on irrigation which is controlled by the state which gives rise to another form of monopoly as only the state can successfully operate an irrigation system.

Beginning about 5,000 years ago there was an uptake of trade on a global level beginning in the middle Asia interaction sphere with lively trade by land and by sea between Mesopotamia, Persia, the Arabian Peninsula and South Asia. With the establishment of empires during the Iron Age the level of trade increased. Among the more prominent overland trade routes were those of the Greeks under Alexander the Great, those of the Romans, the Royal Persian Road and the Chinese trade routes beginning with the Han dynasty and known as the Silk Road which existed from approximately 200 BCE to 1453 CE. The next increase in global trade occurred with the Maritime revolution in Europe starting in the 15th Century that allowed trade between the Old World and the New World. The traders formed monopolies with the rulers of the state as participants in the trading cartels. This led in time, to colonialism and mercantilism, a form of economic monopoly of the colonizing states over the peoples of the territories they colonized.

Another factor contributing to monopolies was the institution of currencies in the form of coin of the realm. The economy of peasants and craftsmen operating in the late Middle Ages made use of market or local currencies such as grain receipts or receipts for goods and services rendered. This system of local currencies allowed the farmers and craftsman, the emerging middle class, to prosper at the expense of the aristocracy and the monarch who became jealous of their success. It was at this stage just as the first stirrings of the Renaissance were occurring that the monarchs instituted two regulations that stifled the emerging middle class's burgeoning economy. The first was the introduction of the coin of the realm, a centralized currency or money. The use of local currencies was outlawed (Rushkoff 2016). Money has two functions: One is the storage of wealth (coin of the realm) and the other is the facilitation of commerce and the exchange of goods and services (which local currencies previously facilitated). The second constraint on commerce was the establishment of monopolistic chartered trading companies by order of the King. The King, by the way, was given a share of these companies. This was the beginning of business people bribing the rulers who operated the government of the realm.

These two developments represented a change of the operating system of the economy and the emergence of capitalism. The medieval economy based on the barter and exchange in the bazaar were replaced by an economy based on money, the centralized currency based on the value of precious metals of gold and silver and dominated by monopolistic corporations chartered or licensed by the crown. This created a hardship for farmers and craftsmen who were required to borrow money and pay interest to conduct their commerce. This hardship resulted in their loss of their former prosperity. This was the beginning of the 1% versus the 99%. Because craftsmen were no longer able to sell the goods they created in order to survive they had to sell their labour. As a result, they only realize a fraction of the value they created and they became wage slaves.

With the industrial revolution another form of monopoly arose replacing the chartered corporations. Manufacturing corporations arose in which the possession of capital was essential and a requirement to start a business to purchase the tools needed for the manufacture of the goods to be produced. These industrial corporations were capitalized by the wealthy as shareholders to whom the management of the company had to answer. The objective of these companies was growth often by acquisition of smaller organizations until they could monopolize a particular market segment. Applying McLuhan's Laws of the Media (McLuhan M. & E. 1988) these industrial corporations enhanced the power of capital, obsolesced the bazaar or local economies based on barter and reduced the influence of the landed aristocracy, retrieved global empires and flipped into personhood, where under the law corporations were given the same rights as individuals but not the same responsibilities.

Rushkoff (2016) in his book *Throwing Rocks at the Google Bus* pointed out because of their mandate for growth to insure a return on the capital of their investors, the corporations looked to create monopolies. The mechanism to create a monopoly by a manufacturer, who was dominant in a certain sector for which there was a strong demand, was to lower their prices to force their competitors to do the same. They continued to lower their prices until their weaker competitors were forced out of business. Once this was accomplished they then increased their price to a level higher than when they had competitors to the disadvantage of the consumer.

Another form of monopoly is the corporate trust in which a number of related corporations form a conglomerate and thereby control the market for some good or service. The first such corporate trust was that of Standard Oil organized by John D. Rockefeller. The abuse of corporate trusts resulted in legislation in certain jurisdictions, such as the Sherman Anti-Trust Act in the United States, to limit the power of these monopolies. Another target of the Sherman Act was the American Tobacco Company in the same year as that Standard Oil was targeted. In more recent times Microsoft was sued by the U. S. government for violating the Sherman Act because it controlled both the operating system and the software of all personal computers other than Apple computers. After a prolonged negotiation Microsoft was force to share its application programming interfaces with other software companies.

Microsoft is only one example of digital age monopolies; the other four being Amazon, Apple, Facebook and Google. One of the factors that has contributed to the emergence of these mega monopolies has been the emergence of the Internet and the World Wide Web. Of this group Facebook is the only one that is primarily a social media company, while the others have various connections to social media. Google and Microsoft own social media companies (YouTube and Skype respectively), Apple provides the hardware platforms for social media and Amazon that depends on the Internet to facilitate its commerce integrates social media into its marketing strategy in a major way. Today's digital mega monopolies are even more dominant in their respective markets than the industrial age monopolies because of the global nature of their business and the interconnectedness of the Internet.

References

Johnson, Allen W., and Timothy Earle. 1987. *The Evolution of Human Societies: From Foraging Group to Agrarian State.* Stanford: Stanford University Press.

Logan, Robert K. 2007. *The Extended Mind: The Emergence of Language, the Human Mind and Culture.* Toronto: University of Toronto Press.

McLuhan, Marshall, and Eric McLuhan. 1988. *Laws of Media: The New Science.* Toronto: University of Toronto Press.

Rushkoff, Douglas. 2016. *Throwing Rocks at the Google Bus.* New York: Portfolio/Penguin.

PART III

SOCIAL MEDIA AND MONOPOLIES

CHAPTER SEVENTEEN

The Rise of Mega Monopolies in the Digital Age

The Future Ain't What It Used to Be

At the beginning of the Internet/World Wide Web revolution, we along with many others, believed that the Internet would have a decentralizing effect and bring an end to monopolies in communications because everyone on the Net would have the ability to communicate to a global audience. The reverse has happened; the digital monopolies are bigger than the pre-digital industrial monopolies. This is certainly the case with Amazon, Apple, Facebook, Google, and Microsoft.

Corey Anton (2018) traced our optimism regarding the liberating effects of the Internet and the World Wide Web way back to McLuhan's observations of the effects of electric media, when Corey wrote:

> McLuhan is, in some ways, a main culprit in helping people imagine that democracy was going to be inherently spread by the decentralizing character of electric media. He did not say as much, but his main claim that electric technologies decentralize led many people to assume that the new media were just by definition, or by inherent character, more democratic, more bottom-up, than traditional print-based hierarchies. And, admittedly, there were senses that some of the platforms seemed that way from the beginning.

One of us (RKL), back in 2000, wrote: "The Internet and the World Wide Web have played a prominent role in the breakdown of Industrial Era monopolies of knowledge by providing a medium whereby non-professionals have been able to share their experiences and network their knowledge (Logan 2004, 60)." This was not the best prediction ever made. We have seen with time as the Net and the Web evolved that for users to gain the access to a global audience and to access the world of information they have to deal with one or more of these mega monopolies. The information that the users generate using these services are captured by and exploited by these digital mega monopolies and used to their advantage at the expense of their users. The World Wide Web becomes a web in which its users are ensnared and their information is exploited by the mega monopolies for their profit and growth.

The Flip: From Media as Extension of Man to Man as Extensions of Their Digital Media

In his book *Understanding Media: Extensions of Man*, McLuhan (1964) suggested that all media, all technologies are merely extensions of our bodies or our psyches. He wrote, "all media are extensions of some human faculty—psychic or physical (McLuhan & Fiore 1967)." He also wrote, "technologies are merely extensions of ourselves (McLuhan 1967, 261)."

The reader should be aware that when McLuhan uses the term 'man' in the subtitle of his book *Understanding Media: Extensions of Man* back in 1964, he was using the term man in its generic sense of humankind or humanity, as was the practice of his day. We have used the term 'man,' fully cognizant that it may prove offensive to some, which is not our intent, but as a play on the words of McLuhan's title. We have taken McLuhan's term extensions of man and flipped media and man and modified media to read as digital media to characterize man as extensions of their digital media rather than McLuhan's media as extensions of man.

McLuhan was not the first to regard technology or our tools as extensions of our bodies. This idea can be traced back to Ralph Waldo Emerson (1875) who wrote: "all the tools and engines on earth are only extensions of man's limbs and senses." Henry Ward Beecher (1887) developed a similar idea: "a tool is but the extension of a man's hand and a machine is but a complex tool." Whether McLuhan was aware of Emerson's and Beecher's idea of tools as extensions of man or whether he developed this idea on his own we will never know. But one thing for certain is that it became a central theme in McLuhan's (1964) understanding of media

THE RISE OF MEGA MONOPOLIES IN THE DIGITAL AGE | 133

and technology and their effects as the following excerpts from *Understanding Media: Extensions of Man* reveals.

> This is merely to say that the personal and social consequences of any medium-- that is, of any *extension of ourselves* -- result from the new scale that is introduced into our affairs by each *extension of ourselves*, or by any new technology ...

> Physiologically, man in the normal use of technology (*or his variously extended body*) is perpetually modified by it and in turn finds ever new ways of modifying his technology. Man becomes, as it were, the sex organs of the machine world, as the bee of the plant world, enabling it to fecundate and to evolve ever new forms. The machine world reciprocates man's love by expediting his wishes and desires, namely, in providing him with wealth (ibid., 23 & 55–56).

With Quentin Fiore in *The Medium is The Massage: An Inventory of Effects*, McLuhan returned to this theme when they wrote, "All media are extensions of some human faculty—psychic or physical (McLuhan & Fiore 1967, 26)." McLuhan also touched on this theme with Barrington Nevitt in *Take Today: Executive as Dropout* when they wrote, "Environments work us over and remake us. It is man who is the *content* of and the *message* of the *media*, which are extensions of himself (McLuhan & Nevitt 1972, 90)."

McLuhan's formulation of media as 'extensions of man' which he formulated for the technologies of the oral, literate and electric ages also hold true for the age that he never experienced, the digital age. Although he was aware of mainframe computers he never had a chance to observe the effects of the personal computer, the Internet or the World Wide Web as he passed away in 1980 before any of these developments had occurred. His insights into electric media, however, allowed him to predict many of the features of digital technology. In a certain sense he seemed to predict the coming of the Internet, Wikipedia and Google.

For example, he spoke of computers providing us information or 'data of a saleable kind,' which is precisely what we do when we pay for the information we access by looking at the advertisements that accompanies the saleable data. He summed this idea in 1979 when he wrote:

> A computer as a research and communication instrument could enhance retrieval, obsolesce mass library organization, retrieve individual encyclopaedic function and flip into a private line to speedily tailored data of a saleable kind (McLuhan 1995, 295–96).

The retrieval of encyclopaedic organization is precisely what the World Wide Web achieves with Wikipedia and Encyclopaedia Britannica. Britannica announced in 2012 it would no longer produce a print version of its encyclopaedia, but would focus exclusively on its online version. There is also a myriad of special-ized online encyclopaedias on various topics and in various languages. There are over 300 versions of Wikipedia in a variety of different languages many of which represent languages that do not have a printed version of an encyclopaedia.

The flip or the reversal was a basic element of McLuhan's technique of analysing media, as the fourth element in his Laws of Media (LOM). Applying the Laws of Media to digital media, we discover that:

- Digital media **enhance** interactivity, access to information and two-way communication.
- They **obsolesce** mass media, like television and newspapers.
- They **retrieve** community.
- And pushed far enough they **flip or reverse** into hyperreality or the loss of con-tact with nature and our bodies. They also flip into global mega-monopolies.

With digital media there is another flip or reversal, namely the reversal of the notion that media are extensions of man. McLuhan divided human commu-nications into the oral era, the written or literate era and the electric era. With digital technology especially, that of the Internet and the World Wide Web we have entered the digital era. Digital technology pushes electric technology to its extreme which causes another flip or reversal, namely that media as extensions of man flips into humans as an extension of digital technology. The flip is that in ad-dition to digital media acting as extensions of a human's psyche as is the case with oral, written and electric media, it is also the case that humans, the users of digital media actually become an extension of their digital technology in the sense that the data they input into digital media becomes an extension of those media.

Culkin (1967), a colleague of McLuhan, wrote that 'we shape our tools and thereafter they shape us.' Culkin's formulation is basically equivalent to McLuhan's (1964, 55–56) remark, that man 'is perpetually modified by it, [his technology].' With digital media there is the added feature that the use of the digital media that we originally shaped is in turn reshaped through our use of those media by capturing our data. Culkin's one liner becomes we shape our digital tools and thereafter we reshape them as we use them.

Here is how digital media such as Facebook and Google are exploiting their users and making them extensions of their technology. Digital media systems con-sist of three elements: there is the hardware and the software of which they are composed and there is a third component, namely, the data that is stored within them. Much of the big data that sits within these systems comes directly from the users of their system as every key stroke and choice the users make is information that is fed into their system as described in *Throwing Rocks at the Google Bus* by Doug Rushkoff (2016, 90–91):

> Projects such as IBM's Watson or Google's Machine Learning lab are not augmenting human intelligence so much as creating systems that think for themselves. With every keystroke and mouse click we make, their algorithms learn more about us while simultaneously becoming more complex than we—or anyone — can comprehend. They are getting smarter while we humans are getting relatively, or perhaps absolutely, dumber. Our machines slowly learn how to manipulate us. It's a field now called captology: the study of how computers and interfaces can influence human behavior.

The users receive the 'speedily tailored data of a saleable kind (McLuhan 1995, 295–96),' described above and pay for it with their attention and reaction to the advertisements that accompanies them. Unbeknownst to them, the data associated with their reactions that they provide literally become an extension of that information system with which they, the users, are interacting. This is the way in which the users become an extension of the system providing them with the information they request. The user literally becomes part of the content of the media with which they interact.

The content McLuhan refers to in his one liner, 'the user is the content' is not the same as the content usurped by the system. The content referred to in McLuhan's one-liner is the interpretation by the user of the information that any medium transmits whether or not it is digital. In other words, the content of a medium referred to in McLuhan's one-liner is not an invariant but depends on the interpretation of the user that is the recipient of the content. In the case where the user becomes an extension of the medium, the system itself is interpreting and storing the reaction to the information it sends to the user by analyzing the user's response. Every keystroke by the user is interpreted by the system and literally becomes part of the content of that system in its data bank. This is the way we become an extension of that medium something McLuhan (1964, 64) prophesized when he wrote: "In this electronic age we see ourselves being translated more and more into the form of information, moving toward the technological extension of consciousness."

What are the implications of this reversal as we become an extension of our digital media? This cybernetic feedback loop traps us and we are at the mercy of the creators and controllers of these digital information systems with which we interact. Big Brother is literally watching us and manipulating us. And we are facilitating their surveillance every time we use Google, Facebook or any of the myriad of social media apps at our disposal.

The warning that McLuhan and Fiore (1967, 26) made about pre-digital media becomes even more so the case with digital media in the age of the Internet and Social Media:

> All media work us over completely. They are so persuasive in their personal, political, economic, aesthetic, psychological, moral, ethical and social consequences that they leave no part of us untouched, unaffected, unaltered. The medium is the massage.

How Do Digital Media Work Us over?

But the control of digital media is even more insidious than 'just working us over' because it is about us personally, it is an invasion of our privacy as we become 'an item in a data bank:'

> As information itself becomes the largest business in the world, data banks know more about individual people than the people do themselves. The more the data banks record about each one of us, the less we exist (McLuhan & Watson 1970, 12)

> Electronic man wears his brain outside his skull and his nervous system on top of his skin. He is like an exposed spider squatting in a thrumming web. But he is not flesh and blood; he is an item in a data bank, ephemeral, easily forgotten and resentful of that fact (McLuhan & Power 1989, 94).

It is interesting that McLuhan uses the term thrumming web long before Tim Berners Lee coined the term the World Wide Web in 1989. The web is also an apt term to describe the way we and our data are entrapped in the World Wide Web like insects caught in a spider's web.

What McLuhan identified before the advent of the Internet of the insidious effect of data banks is an even greater problem today as Rushkoff has pointed out in his book Throwing Rocks at the Google Bus, "This is *Google's model of giving away everything in return for looking at their ads and sharing all our data* ... Digital industrialism turns human data into the new commodity—Rushkoff (2016, 37 & 44)."

The potential for their abuse of our data is greater with the digital technology companies such as Amazon, Apple, Facebook, Google and Microsoft because of their monopolistic nature. Before the advent of the digital monopolies when our technologies were only extensions of us we were more or less in control of them. Certainly, those tools affected us but they were not used by others to control us. That is no longer the case with digital media because those that control digital information systems can use the data we key into their systems to manipulate us. The field of captology has the direct aim of manipulating our behavior in terms of what we purchase and even how we vote by making use of what they learn about us. BJ Fogg (http://captology.stanford.edu/resources/thoughts-onpersuasive-technology.html, accessed December 17, 2019), who coined the term captology described its effects in the following terms:

> After we ran a number of experiments, and after these studies were replicated else-where, the results were undeniable. Computers could indeed be designed to influence people, to change their thoughts and behaviors … Today, we are surrounded by per-suasive technologies. Everywhere that digital media touches our lives, more and more there is an element of persuasion; a design created by humans and implemented in code to influence what we think, and more and more, what we do …

> Today, we are surrounded by persuasive technologies. Everywhere that digital media touches our lives, more and more there is an element of persuasion; a design created by humans and implemented in code to influence what we think, and more and more, what we do. We are surrounded. Persuasive technology is in our living rooms, in our cars. When we communicate with our loved ones online, through Facebook, persua-sion is there. When we withdraw money from the bank at the ATM, an element of persuasion may be there. When we purchase a gift online for a birthday, once again, we are being exposed to persuasion. In fact, we carry a persuasive platform, the mobile phone, with us most everywhere we go.

McLuhan Reversals Created by Digital Monopolies

There is the danger we face as we become extensions of our digital technologies rather than the other way around as was the case with our pre-digital technologies when our technologies were merely extensions of us. This in spite of the promise that the Internet would allow us to be part of a two-way channel of communi-cation. The mega monopolies we identified above and many other smaller ones dominate the activities of the Internet. It was not the original intention of those like Tim Berners Lee to create such dominant behemoths. It is, however, the natural character of digital media to aggregate and when this is coupled with the natural tendency for growth in a capitalistic system in which investors de-mand a return on their investments, the result is the mega monopolies we have identified and the many of the smaller ones that dominate online activities and commerce.

Not only have digital media and especially social media given us greater ac-cess to information, but have given others greater access to our informa-tion and greater access to us by exploiting our data. Google and the social media companies like Facebook have two level of customers, the users like us who pay with our attention and our information and the customers that pay with cash to these companies in order to access our attention and our information.

Although the mega monopolies are providing a service that their users find useful and desirable there is always the possibility of malevolent action when so much power is concentrated in the hands of a small number of agents, which is exactly what happen with Facebook. While not intending to interfere in the American 2016 presidential election or the Brexit referendum in the United Kingdom that is exactly what agents did making use of the infrastructure that Facebook created. We will explore this and other abuses of social media in the next chapter.

More Reversals with Digital Media

In addition to the reversal where the user becomes the extension of the digital media instead of the medium being an extension of the user as McLuhan suggested, there are some additional flips or reversals with digital media. Our tools or media comprise the environment or ground in which we operate which is still true with digital media but we, the users of digital media, become the ground in which digital media operate as their effectiveness depends on the information ground that we, their users create and provide them unknowingly. So, we have the flip of digital media operating in the information ground of their users in addition to their users operating in the ground of their digital media. The feedback of the users become the feedforward for the digital media. McLuhan's one liner, 'the content of any new medium is another older medium' flips into the content of any new digital medium is the personal data of its users or visitors. McLuhan' one-liner, "societies imitate their technologies" flips into 'technologies imitate their societies'. As the personal data of the users of a digital medium become part of its content, rather than societies imitating their technology, we now have the reverse in that digital media or technologies now imitate their users.

McLuhan's signature one-liner 'the medium is the message' reverses into 'the user is the message' as the user's information becomes the content of the digital medium. That information is then tailored to exploit the needs, interests and desires of those users to the advantage of the operators or owners of the digital medium as well as the customers of that digital medium who use the data they purchase for their own commercial or political interests. Not only are the effects of digital media subliminal like all other media but the appropriation of the user's data is also subliminal in that the user is unaware of the process. In addition to the visitor to an Internet site becoming a user of the site, the site becomes a user of the visitor. Just as there is no privacy in a village it is also the case that there is no privacy in the global village of the Internet. Finally, there is a new reversal of cause and effect in that the effect of users using a Web site becomes the cause of the Web site using the visitors' data and eventually using the users.

Monopolies of Knowledge in the Digital Age

Harold Innis (1951, 1972) defined a monopoly of knowledge as pertaining to a ruling class that could maintain political or economic power by their exclusive use or control of a vital communication technology. In the oral era it was the bards, the singers of tales, that had a monopoly of knowledge through their ability to memorize their epic poems and their rhetorical ability to use spoken language persuasively. In the literate age before universal education those that possessed the skills of literacy were able to dominate those that were illiterate. In the age of print those that possessed or controlled a printing press could dominate their society. One of the examples of this that Innis alluded to was the dominance of the Hearst newspaper chain in setting the agenda for the foreign policy of the United States at the very end of the 19th Century.

The fears that Innis expressed in 1951 have abated somewhat because computing and connectivity have led to more open systems in which information is free to flow and small elites are no longer as able to completely control the creation of wealth and the flow of information. The Internet and the World Wide Web have played a prominent role in the breakdown of Industrial Era monopolies of knowledge by providing a medium whereby non-professionals have been able to share their experiences and network their knowledge. Web sites that act as electronic support groups have sprung up all over the Net providing practical suggestions for those who have to cope with a variety of different political, economic, medical, psychological and social problems. Bloggers represent a further evolution of this trend not only for political opinion but also for support and information for a variety of interests and concerns. The Internet cuts two ways; it provides both service and disservice as McLuhan long ago observed: "All I am saying is that any product or innovation creates both service and disservice environments which reshape human attitudes (Molinaro, McLuhan, & Toye 1987, 404)."

The universal access to information and the ability to share one's opinion is a service side of these digital media monopolies. To see the disservice side of these mega-monopolistic companies like Google, Facebook, and Amazon one must take into account that they have created a new form of the monopoly of knowledge. By harvesting the personal data of their users these companies without the permission of their users bombard those users with targeted ads, a practice which is clearly a disservice as pointed out by Shoshana Zuboff (2019) in her book *Surveillance Capitalism: The Fight for a Human Future at the New Frontier of Power*. And just as McLuhan suggested the media that these mega monopolies make use of provide both service and disservice.

References

Anton, Corey. 2018. "Comments on "How to Fix Facebook," MEA convention 2018. Presentation at the 2018 Media Ecology Convention in Orono Maine. Private communication in an email entitled "MEA follow-up" that Corey Anton sent to Bob Logan on July 11, 2018.

Beecher, Henry Ward. 1887. *Proverbs from Plymouth Pulpit*. Berlin: Theclassics.us.

Culkin, John. 1967. 'A Schoolman's Guide to Marshall McLuhan', *Saturday Review* (March 18, 1967): 51–53, 71–72.

Emerson, Ralph Waldo. 1875. *Society and Solitude: Twelve Chapters*. Boston: James R. Osgood and Company.

Innis, Harold. 1951. *The Bias of Communication*. Toronto: Univ. of Toronto Press.

Innis, Harold. 1972. *Empire and Communications*. With foreword by Marshall McLuhan. Originally pub. by Oxford Univ. Press [1950]. Toronto: Univ. of Toronto Press.

Logan, Robert K. 2004. *The Sixth Language: Learning a Living in the Internet Age*. Caldwell NJ: Blackburn Press (1st edition, 2000). Toronto: Stoddart Publishing.

McLuhan, Marshall. 1964. *Understanding Media: Extensions of Man*. New York: McGraw Hill. (The page references in the text are for the McGraw Hill paperback second edition. Readers should be aware that the pagination in other editions is different.)

McLuhan, Marshall. 1967. "Interview." In *McLuhan, Hot & Cool*, edited by Gerald E. Stearn. New York: Dial Press.

McLuhan, Marshall. 1995. "I. About Media." In *Essential McLuhan*, edited by Eric McLuhan and Frank Zingrone. Concord Ontario: Anansi.

McLuhan, Marshall, and Quentin Fiore. 1967. *The Medium is the Massage: An Inventory of Effects*. New York: Random House.

McLuhan, Marshall, and Watson, Wilfred. 1970. *From Cliché to Archetype*. New York: Viking.

McLuhan, Marshall, and Barrington Nevitt. 1972. *Take Today: The Executive as Dropout*. Toronto: Longman Canada.

Molinaro, M. C. McLuhan & W. Toye 1987. *Letters of Marshall McLuhan*. Toronto: Oxford University Press.

Rushkoff, Douglas. 2016. *Throwing Rocks at the Google Bus*. New York: Portfolio/Penguin.

Zuboff, Shoshana. 2019. *Surveillance Capitalism: The Fight for a Human Future at the New Frontier of Power*.

CHAPTER EIGHTEEN

Digital Age Monopolies and Social Media

Introduction

The interaction of the digital age monopolies and social media is complex. In this chapter we will describe two forms of this interaction, namely

1. the monopolistic character of a number of social media apps including: Facebook, Instagram, Snapchat, Reddit, Tinder, Twitter and YouTube
2. the interaction of a number of digital mega monopolies with social media including Amazon, Apple, Google and Microsoft

The monopolies in the digital age including those of social media are slightly different than the definition of a monopoly in the pre-digital era. A monopoly is defined as a

> market situation where one producer (or a group of producers acting in concert) controls supply of a good or service, and where the entry of a new producer is prevented or highly restricted. Monopolist firms (in their attempt to maximize profits) keep the price high and restrict the output, and show little or no responsiveness to the needs of their customers (http://www.businessdictionary.com/definition/monopoly.html accessed on March 2, 2020).

This is not how monopolies are created in the digital age including social media apps. The reason for this is that the services in the digital age must be able to work with the other users of those services. What happens in the digital age is that the popularity of an operating system or a software package or an app sets a standard and because there is a need for compatibility this leads to an effective monopoly. The initial success of Apple computers and then of IBM personal computers set two standards for operating systems creating a virtual monopoly for Apple's MacOS and Microsoft's MS Dos/Windows.

What was true for the operating systems of MacOS and MS Dos/Windows is also true for the software apps that are compatible with these two operating systems. A similar dynamic exists for social media where linking with friends and associates is facilitated by using the same social media app. Once a social media app sets a standard and a critical mass of users, other users new to social media will flock to that particular app and those on a less popular app will migrate to the new app. A classic example of a migration from an older to a newer app was the migration of many MySpace users to Facebook. The main difference in the dynamics of the pre-digital and the digital monopolies is that in the former the consumer is forced to deal with the monopoly whereas in the digital case the users choose to use the dominant or the most desirable app and hence create the monopoly by their desire to be with the app that provides them with the most links to others.

As we will discover later in this chapter the way new social media apps emerged despite the dominance of Facebook was by providing a new feature or a focus on a new segment of potential social media users. For example, by catering to the needs of business professionals and academics LinkedIn was able to find a market segment despite the dominance of Facebook. Flickr and then Instagram found their niche with a focus on sharing photographs and YouTube and Vimeo by sharing videos. Twitter's niche was micro blogging and Tinder thrived as a dating site. But even in the dating site space other players found a niche by appealing to specific communities based on ethnicity, religion, or sexual orientation.

The Social Media Monopolies

Of the social media monopolies, Facebook founded in 2004 is the one mega monopoly that has completely dominated its field reducing its competitors, Friendster, founded in 2002, and MySpace, founded in 2003, to relative oblivion. LinkedIn is another general social media site like Facebook but it caters to professionals, business folks and academics and styles itself as "the world's largest professional community." It has features, that this audience appreciate such as an easy way to share their work experience, accomplishments and publications.

In addition to Facebook we will also examine those social media that have created a monopoly or a near monopoly in their particular social media niche. Examples include the following:

1. Twitter that owns the microblogging space that limits the messaging to 280 characters (which was 140 characters prior to November 7, 2017).
2. Instagram and Flickr where they specialize in sharing photos and videos with Instagram dominating Flickr because it incorporates social media linking capabilities within its app;
3. Snapchat where they specialize in sharing messages, photos and videos that quickly disappear;
4. Reddit where their specialty is sharing news of and stories about a large class of topic and discussions of those news items and stories;
5. Dating sites including Tinder that serves the general population and those that serve various specialized niche communities where the focus is on ethnicity, religion or sexual orientation.
6. YouTube by and large monopolizes the video sharing space but in which there is room for other players of which Vimeo is the most prominent.

Facebook: A Mega Monopoly

With nearly 2.7 Billion users as of the 2nd quarter of 2020 Facebook (FB) is perhaps the largest monopoly ever created in terms of users/customers. In additions to its users with a FB presence here is also the millions of advertisers that buy ads on Facebook making it with Google one of the world's largest sellers of advertisements. "In the second quarter of 2020, Facebook announced that over nine million active advertisers were using the social networking platform to promote their products and services (https://www.statista.com/statistics/778191/active-facebook-advertisers/, accessed February 1, 2021)." In addition to paid advertising 80 million businesses have a page on Facebook (https://www.oberlo.com/blog/facebook-statistics, accessed February 1, 2021).

What makes Facebook such a desirable venue for advertising is that the advertiser is able to target the recipient of the ads based on their previous activities on Facebook. Many other social media as well as Google also target their users with advertising based on their previous history on their site. This capability has led to abuse by political operatives to affect the outcomes of democratic elections and referenda in a number of countries including the American 2016 presidential election and the British Brexit referendum to name just two.

According to an article entitled "5 of the Biggest Controversies and Criticisms Facing Facebook" posted on http://mediakix.com/2017/05/facebook-controversy-criticism-history/#gs.o=DrseI accessed on February 1, 2021 the following problems with Facebook have been identified: "1. Fake Accounts & Ad Fraud on Facebook; 2. Facebook's Video Metric Miscalculation; 3. Facebook Live's Violence Problem; 4. The Rise of Fake News and 5. Continued Controversy Over Censorship & Facebook's Algorithm."

In addition to these there is also

1. Facebook's sale of data to agents that misuse it such as was the case with Cambridge Analytica.
2. Promotion of addiction to its site using the captology techniques of Fogg and Eyal mentioned in Chapter Six.

MySpace

The focus of MySpace has been on entertainment and music, which accounted for its initial success but also led to its being eclipsed by Facebook. Although MySpace started a year before Facebook in 2003 and was initially the most popular social media site in the world it was eclipsed by Facebook in 2008 after which its number of users steadily declined so that as of the end of 2018 its number of users was approximately 50 million compared to the 75.9 million users it had at its peak in December of 2008 and quite small when compared with Facebook's 2.5 billion users. MySpace, however, is still a force to be reckoned with in the space of music artists and entertainers. There are 14.2 million artists on MySpace, 53 million songs, and 300 million monthly video views (https://expandedramblings.com/index.php/myspace-stats-then-now/ accessed Feb. 28, 2019).

LinkedIn

LinkedIn, a subsidiary of Microsoft, has a mini-monopoly when it comes to professional and academic social media networking with 675 million registered users in 200 countries of which 310 million or so are active. Its main source of income comes from selling the information of recruiters and sales professionals (https://www.omnicoreagency.com/linkedin-statistics/, accessed March 11, 2020).

Academic Pre-print Sites that also Function as Social Media

There are also a number of Web sites that provide academics a way to share their pre-prints and published articles with their respective research communities. Here is a list of such sites and the communities they cater to:

- Academia.edu caters to the general academic community.
- Researchgate.net also caters to the general academic community.
- Google Scholar also caters to the general academic community.
- arXiv caters to the mathematics, physics, astronomy, electrical engineering, computer science, quantitative biology, statistics, mathematical finance and economics academic communities.
- IEEE Xplore caters to the engineering and technology communities.
- ScienceDirect caters to the physical sciences and engineering, life sciences, health sciences, and social sciences and humanities communities.
- Social Science Research Network (SSRN) caters to the social science community.
- Scribd is not an academic site but it caters to the community of writers as well as publishers who sell their publications on the site.

Specialized General Facebook-Like Social Media

There are numerous specialized general Facebook-like social media sites that are organized to cater to the citizens of a particular country, which in the case of China or Russia can be quite large. Others social media sites are organized around a particular activity, interest, activism concern, shared ethnic identity, sexual orientation, profession, online collaboration and gaming. For a detailed list of these sites see the Appendix.

The Instagram Monopoly

Instagram a social media site that specializes in the sharing of photos and videos is not exactly a monopoly because of Flickr. Instagram at 1 billion users has 10 times the number of users even though it started in October of 2010 versus Flickr's February 2004 launch. Although the two apps both store photographs and videos they each have a different focus (pun unintended). Flickr outshines Instagram for those serious about photography as it has many more editing assets than Instagram; better ways to organize one's photos and 30 seconds for videos views versus 15 seconds for Instagram. Instagram, however, is much better at the socializing aspect of sharing photographs. Instagram, like Facebook that owns it, does a great job with the social dimension of photo sharing with its features such as likes; sending posts; Instagram Stories; seeing photos that one is tagged in; links to social network accounts; link to photos that you 'liked'; and seeing posts on a world map.

The Snapchat Monopoly

Even though Snapchat is an app for sharing photos and other forms of multimedia like Instagram and Flickr, it has created a monopoly or a niche for itself by adding the unique feature that the materials that are shared disappear after a short time (one to ten seconds as specified by the poster).

The Reddit Monopoly

Reddit is a social news aggregator based in the USA that completely dominates its genre with 234 million unique users, 542 million monthly visitors, ranking as the #6 most visited website in U.S., #5 in Canada and #18 in the world (www.alexa. com, accessed March 1, 2020). The only competition to Reddit in a look-a-like site Voat that a number of Reddit users that were banned by Reddit for questionable content migrated to. Voat which operates under the mantra of freedom of speech has allowed certain racist groups to post to its site. Voat has not been a great success financially and has experienced some difficulty meeting its financial obligations.

Dating Site Monopolies

Tinder completely dominates this category with some competition from specialized dating sites organized along religion, ethnicity and sexual orientation.

The Twitter Monopoly

Twitter has a monopoly of the microblogging space where microblogging is a combination of a blog and instant messaging that can be posted to and shared with an audience online where there are restrictions on the length of the post such as Twitter's original restriction to 140 characters later increased to 280 characters on November 7, 2017. Tumblr provides some competition to Twitter in the microblogging space as many of the posts on Tumblr are short and can be characterized as microblogs. However, because there are no restrictions on length Tumblr is not technically a microblogging app.

As for the other apps that are microblogs with restrictions on length they never were able to compete with Twitter and many are now defunct as has been explained by Chris Trygstad, Network Director of a Med Device/Health Information Tech Co., whose explanation applies to the dominance of the other monopolies we have been discussing:

> There is/was: Plurk, Jaiku, Pownce, BrightKite, FriendFeed, Identi.ca and many more microblogging platforms. I actually used to be on a number of them, and update my status to Ping.Fm and Hellotxt, which would push to a huge number of these sites. I quit doing so, because no one was on them. Twitter puts out a good product, but more important to their success was the network affect. They gained the critical mass of users to sustain an ecosystem first. There is space for competition, in niches. Short answer, there is competition, but none have the visibility and mindshare that Twitter enjoys (yet) (https://www.quora.com/Why-are-there-no-Twitter-competitors).

The YouTube Monopoly

YouTube with two billion monthly users and one billion hours of videos viewed and 720,000 hours of video uploaded every day (https://www.oberlo.ca/blog/youtube-statistics, accessed February 1, 2021) does not exactly have a monopoly but it is certainly by far the dominant player in sharing videos. YouTube is the second most-visited website in the world after Google Search, according to Alexa Internet rankings. (https://en.wikipedia.org/wiki/YouTube, accessed February 1, 2021).

YouTube does have competitors including Vimeo, Twitch, Dailymotion, Metacafe, Photobucket, Flickr and Veoh. Vimeo with 170 million unique visitors each month and over 90 million registered users is YouTube's closest competitor in the video sharing space (https://www.feedough.com/youtube-vs-vimeo/, accessed February 1, 2021). Their numbers do not even come close to those of YouTube.

Corey Anton (2018) describes his experience with YouTube in its early days and how that all changed when they squeezed out the little guys as they became more successful and achieved the status of a monopoly. He wrote:

> My early experience in YouTube when the platform was only about a year old … was amazing. Anyone could share videos with anyone, and it seemed a pretty level playing

field. But then, things changed for me (and for YouTube too). I met a YouTube 'partner,' and he explained that a 'partner' got profit-sharing from advertising and they were also able to upload videos of any length. To be eligible for partnership, someone needed 2,000 subscribers, and so, that became my mission. By the time I became a partner I was running advertising on my channel and shortly thereafter opened an Amazon seller account. This allowed me to shoot a video on a book, post it on YouTube and attach a link to Amazon, where I then would get a percentage of the sale for the referral. At first, it was really wild and woolly – as an example, I had made a video on a book and I posted a link to it. At this point of Amazon's functionality, my seller ID tag was somehow attached to a shopper's forward browsing from the link. Someone bought an expensive piece of farm equipment, and I made about a hundred dollars commission for the referral! Needless to say, Amazon was pretty quick to change a lot of its policies and protocols for seller ID tags. Simultaneous to this, YouTube's platform kept changing, and often to diminish peer-to-peer interactivity and promote major players interested in purchasing eyeballs. YouTube also kept tightening its revenue-sharing program. Many channels were denied advertising for inappropriate content and bigger and bigger players entered into the scene. Many smaller "youtubers" were squeezed out. Within about a decade from its inception, YouTube was looking more and more like a mega-monopoly and an extension of Google/Amazon.

Blogging Monopolies

There is no particular blogging app that completely monopolizes the blogging space but there are a number of dominant players that users choose according to their individual needs.

Tumblr with 500 million blogs (www.statista.com/statistics/256235/total-cumulative-number-of-tumblr-blogs/, accessed February 1, 2021) has the most users because it appeals to the casual blogger as it is easy to use. It has the additional feature that it is as much a social networking app as it is a blogging platform as it provides a way for bloggers to connect with each other and comment on their respective blogs creating a friendly social media environment. Another reason for the popularity of Tumblr was described on (https://firstsiteguide.com/wordpress-tumblr/, accessed on March 16, 2019) in the following terms: "If you don't like complicated dashboards and user interfaces that require you to spend valuable time on things other than blogging, you will fancy Tumblr. From creating a free account to writing your first post, everything will be ready in just a few clicks."

Google's Blogger is another easy to use blogging app that is owned by Google and integrates easily for those with Google accounts.

WordPress appeals to the serious blogger who is looking for access to large numbers of designs and plugins. It comes in two versions the hosted version

WordPress.com and WordPress.org which involves self-hosting and is the best choice for professional blogs, blogs that are to be used to generate revenue or blogs associated with a business. In addition to being used by bloggers WordPress is a content management system (CMS) that is also used by many to create their own general-purpose Web sites "There are approximately 76.5 million WordPress. com blogs (https://www.codeinwp.com/blog/wordpress-statistics/, accessed Feb. 1, 2021).

There are five additional blogging apps in this crowded space, namely, Medium, Ghost, Squarespace, Joomla and Drupal.

Instant Messaging Monopolies

There is no instant messaging (IM) monopoly although the two most popular IM apps are WhatsApp and FB Messenger both owned by Facebook. The third most popular app is WeChat that operates in China. In fourth place and fifth place are Skype and SnapChat respectively. Kik Messenger, eBuddy, Line and Apple's iMessage are also significant players. All in all, there is no monopoly but one could say that the two Facebook apps dominate this category outside of China.

Digital Monopoly Interactions with Social Media: Amazon, Apple, Google and Microsoft

In this next section we describe the social media strategy of four of the largest digital media mega-monopolies, namely Amazon, Apple, Google and Microsoft. The fifth digital media mega-monopoly, Facebook, has already been described in Chapter Seven.

Amazon and Social Media

Amazon has created a mega-monopoly for online shopping and is becoming the dominant player in retail sales having already forced many retail operations out of business particularly in book trade but also department stores and retail chains like Toys "R" US which closed its 800 US stores as well as it stores in the UK and Canada.

Giselle Ambromovich (2017) has suggested that the reason that Amazon is killing retail operations in many sectors across the globe is because of the following five features of its operations: (1) Two-Day shipping; (2) Inventory efficiencies; (3) Killer product search; (4) Data and personalization; and (5) Customer experience.

We would add a sixth reason for the success of Amazon which is its social media strategy which consists of the following seven elements: (1) its customers reviews, (2) its Facebook page, (3) its use of Twitter, (4) its posts on Pinterest, (5) its posts on Instagram, (6) its partnership with Snapchat and (7) Amazon Spark, the social media app it created for its customers.

1. Customers reviews are essential for Amazon because it is the only way that its customers can learn about the products it is offering for sale online. Amazon shoppers rely on these reviews and so it becomes de facto a form of social media on Amazon.com.
2. Amazon's Facebook page (https://www.facebook.com/Amazon/) which we visited on March 9, 2020 boasted that it had 29,369,071 likes and 28,608,754 followers. The site contains product reviews, customer complaints that are handled respectfully, and many, many promotions.
3. Amazon has partnered with Twitter to drive business to its site. Twitter users can link their accounts to an Amazon account, and automatically add items to the shopping cart by responding to any tweet with an Amazon product link bearing the hashtag #AmazonCart. Customers never leave the Twitter feed, and the product is waiting for them when they head over to Amazon (https://www.cnet.com/news/amazon-twitter-link-up-for-easy-shopping-through-amazoncart/ accessed March 9, 2020.
4. Amazon's Pinterest site https://www.pinterest.ca/amazon/ shows pictures of products with a shop now link that brings one directly to Amazon.com to purchase the item.
5. Amazon's Instagram site can be found at https://www.instagram.com/amazon/?hl=en
6. Amazon Snapchat partnership "Users can use Snapchat's camera to scan a physical object or barcode, which brings up a card showing that item and similar ones along with their title, price, thumbnail image, average review score and Prime availability. When they tap on one, they'll be sent to Amazon's app or site to buy it (https://techcrunch.com/2018/09/24/snapchat-amazon-visual-search/, accessed March 9, 2020).
7. Amazon Spark: Amazon has created a social media app to promote users to shop at Amazon using their smart phone. It is part of the Amazon app for the iPhone and Android. It describes its Spark app as follows:

Amazon Spark is a place to discover things from people who share your interests. Whether you're looking for inspiration for home décor or seeking advice for the best long-distance running shoes, Spark makes it easy to discover—and shop—stories and ideas from a community that likes what you like. (https://www.amazon.com/Spark/b?ie=UTF8&node=16907772011, accessed March 9, 2020).

But then Amazon Spark reminds visitors: "Shop: See something you like? With Spark, you're one tap away from purchasing the products you discover. Tap the shopping bag in the photo and find it on Amazon (ibid.)." They make it so easy to shop. You never have to leave home. And with Spark one can get advice on what to shop for. They proclaim, "Connect: Get advice and feedback from a community of people with similar interests (ibid.)."

Apple and Social Media

Apple has a minimalist approach to social media and one that is unlike any of its competitors as can be judged by some of the titles to articles about Apple's social media strategy. In the article entitled "Apple's totally bizarre social media strategy that makes perfect sense (medium.com/@nick_hessler/apples-totally-bizarre-social-media-strategy-that-makes-perfect-sense-a10d050f4d46 accessed March 9, 2019)" author Nick Hessler wrote:

> Most brands are furiously creating content to stay on the "current trend bandwagon" to attempt to stay relevant in the social atmosphere while also pushing out information about their products. When you actually look at Apple on Facebook and Twitter and you realize they have none of that. All 12,921,598 total followers between the two platforms haven't ever seen a post from the tech giant.

In the article entitled "Inside Apple's odd, yet effective social media strategy (https://www.cio.com/article/2979114/social-networking/inside-apples-odd-yet-effective-social-media-strategy.html accessed March 9, 2020)" author Matt Kapko wrote: "Apple does social media differently than its peers in the tech world, and though it isn't ignoring social to the extent it did in the past, you shouldn't expect to see any official @Apple account on Twitter anytime soon."

The blogger at Analytive.com in a blog post entitled "How Apple is winning on social media" wrote:

> To say that Apple is successful on social media is an understatement … Now you might be thinking, *"Wait a minute! Apple doesn't even use social media!"* And you'd be

mostly correct…They don't have a Twitter feed. They don't have any official Facebook accounts. And yet they are one of the most successful brands in driving buzz across social media (https://analytive.com/blog/apple-winning-social-media, accessed March 9, 2019.)

Google and Social Media

Google has (or had in the case of Google Plus which closed on April 2, 2019) a number of social media apps including Allo, Blogger, Duo, Gmail, Google Groups, Google Hangout, Google Plus, Google Talk and the most successful of all of them, YouTube.

- Allo is an instant messaging app for smartphones that works for both the iPhone and Android devices.
- Blogger is a blogging app.
- Duo is a video chat mobile device for smartphones that works for both the iPhone and Android devices.
- Gmail is a standard email app offered for free by Google with over a billion users.
- Google Groups provides a platform for discussion groups as well as access to Usenet newsgroups.
- Google Hangouts is a platform that combines VoIP, video chat and messaging.
- Google Plus or Google+ was a social network organized along the lines of Facebook that was terminated on April 2, 2019. Although Google Plus tried to emulate Facebook it lacked the important ingredient of familiarity.

  By requiring new Google users to also open Google+ accounts, Google believed it could quickly amass Google+ members simply by getting Gmail users—hundreds of millions at the time—onboard and introducing several Facebook-like features … While Google+ copied Facebook, it lacked the indefinable sense of virtual intimacy Facebook had then. On Facebook, many of those suggested friends were likely real-life friends, family, and coworkers. Google+ lacked that same feeling of familiarity, pulling recommended friends from your Gmail contacts (https://finance.yahoo.com/news/googles-social-network-spectacular-failure-183906984.html accessed March 16, 2019).
- Google Talk was an instant messaging service that is now part of Google Hangouts

- Google Voice is a telephone service that includes voice and text messaging, voicemail services and call forwarding in the U.S. and Canada.
- YouTube is a video sharing app that we have described in Chapter Thirteen.

Microsoft and Social Media

Microsoft's most prominent social media app is Skype (see Chapter Five), which it acquired in May of 2011 for $8.5 billion. Microsoft also acquired LinkedIn (described above and in Chapter Seven), another significant social media app for $26.2 billion in December of 2016.

Microsoft developed an instant messaging client in 1999 that it rebranded in 2005 as MSN Messenger. With the acquisition of Skype, Messenger was combined with Skype and then discontinued in 2013. Microsoft acquired Yammer (a freemium enterprise social networking service) in 2012 for US$1.2 billion. Microsoft launched So.cl, a social network/search service similar to Google Plus in 2012, which they operated until March 15, 2017 when they closed it down due to its lack of success.

Microsoft makes use of social media to promote and support its products and services making use of Facebook, Twitter, Pinterest and formerly making use of Google Plus. On Facebook it has pages for its sub-brands and products in addition to its main corporate page. It has a similar strategy with Twitter accounts for its sub-brands and products.

Conclusion

Digital technology and specifically the Internet and the Web seemed to hold the promise of the possible end of the control by the wealthy of the planet's resources and in particular its channels of communication. It looked like freedom of the press was not going to belong only to those that owned one but with two-way flow of information finally the 99%-ers could find a voice. This has certainly happened. What we did not see was that the two-way flow of information not only allows for self-expression for all (at least for those with access to the Net) but it also allows the large monopolies that dominate the Internet to exploit without our permission the information and data we generate unintentionally while visiting their sites, which is clearly a disservice.

References

Ambromovich, Giselle. 2017. "5 Ways Amazon Has Disrupted Retail—So Far" (https://www.cmo.com/features/articles/2017/10/23/two-ways-amazon-is-disrupting-retail-and-advice-for-the-way-forward.html#gs.K4IHPz0, accessed on March 8, 2019)

Anton, Corey. 2018. "Comments on "How to Fix Facebook," MEA Convention 2018. Presentation at the 2018 Media Ecology Convention in Orono Maine. Private Communication in an Email Entitled "MEA follow-up" that Corey Anton Sent to Bob Logan on July 11, 2018.

CHAPTER NINETEEN

Social Media, Branding and Advertising

Introduction

In this chapter, we identify the emerging trends in social media branding and consider the following questions:

- Why is the brand experience relevant to social media?
- How do brands connect to users through social media?
- How do businesses develop an omnichannel presence by creating social media accounts for their brands and by retaining social media influencers?
- Is our data private or public? What is it being used for? How does user data play a part in targeted advertising?

Brands Are Social Media Users

The users of social media are primarily individuals with personal accounts but a significant other set of social media users are brands, whose use of social media we will explore. To promote their brands, companies have created a multichannel or omnichannel presence on several social media platforms to connect with audiences wherever they may be. The presence of brands takes three forms: i. straight advertising; ii. a social media account on behalf of the brand on a particular social media app; iii. the recruitment of social media influencers that endorse the product on their social media sites and hence promote the brand.

We may therefore think of brands as users, just like us individuals. One difference, however, is that companies create business transaction accounts and customer acquisition features that link to external websites (i.e. digital realms outside of the social media platforms themselves) where products or services can be purchased. The major players in social media advertising are Facebook and Instagram, a subsidiary of Facebook since 2012. These platforms host personal accounts and business accounts in a unified space, connecting users to relevant brands based on their personal data via targeted marketing. Targeted ads will be further explained later in this chapter, as they play a large part in the relationship of users with brands that we see on social media today. Having a social media account makes brands more accessible and explorable, even more so than the promotion of a brand in physical stores. Despite presenting themselves as users, just like the rest of us, brands on social media have an ulterior motive for being 'social'. Businesses are on social media platforms to market products, services, and lifestyles to users by way of a personalized strategy that increases the access to their brands.

Brands act like users and hop on Internet trends to be more relatable, authentic, and organize their site to avoid exposing their ulterior marketing motive for being on social media. They retweet viral memes and post socially relevant content in order to provide their audience with an enjoyable experience that integrates with the brand's overall social media strategy. Brands' social media accounts are used primarily to show face and be present in the digital world. There was an obvious social barrier between businesses and customers before social media boomed. Now, brands have found a way to break that barrier and participate in the social space on the same terms as their targeted users. They need users to like them in order to be successful and market their products on personal digital platforms, so they integrate themselves and try to look less like salespeople and more like sympathetic friends. This organic reach, as opposed to paid reach and sponsored content, primarily depends on user approval and engagement with the branded content. Paid ads and brands buying their way into users' feeds are effective methods of social media popularity, but ultimately, organic engagement and brand loyalty is what lasts in the digital status quo. It is well known that advertising and other forms of promotion are as much about retaining customers as it is about finding new customers.

Users determine brand popularity in the social media community. Metrics used to assess this user-brand relationship are both quantitative (social media engagement, likes, reach, impressions) and qualitative (what audiences are tweeting about or to the brand, i.e. the brand's user feedback). Quantitative metrics are provided by Facebook and Instagram analytics platforms cyclically, showing brands what's working with their audience and what isn't in terms of hard cold facts. There's no doubt that quantitative analysis is indicative of brands' social standing on these platforms, but qualitative metrics are, arguably, just as important.

After Snapchat's user experience (UX) redesign in 2018, Kylie Jenner, a major influencer tweeted "does anyone else not open Snapchat anymore? or is it just me?", and the company's market value dropped by a considerable amount in no time. Keep in mind, Snapchat isn't just any brand, it's a whole platform that hosts multi-branded content. Kylie Jenner, granted, isn't just any user—she has millions of followers and is a brand herself. Snapchat got a lot of backlash for their redesign online, both from influencers and general users, yet they didn't revert back to their original design. Naturally, they suffered for it and became irrelevant after being one of the most used social media in 2017. All it took was users deciding Snapchat wasn't serving their social media experience well anymore.

Trends in Social Media Branding

Lucidity, concision, authenticity, relatability and transparency promote better user experience (UX). Users tend to engage more with brands that communicate transparently and are easily accessible both visually and textually. Homogeneous design trends have dominated e-commerce platforms and their linked social media accounts. Businesses that have gone digital, post content in the form of infographics and videos in order to present information in the most digestible way. Users tend to decide whether they are staying on a page or exploring a brand further within 3 seconds of exposure, so visual aids have become the dominant trend in UX design on social media and e-commerce websites. This trend goes hand in hand with the transparency trend—people want to know what a brand is about without having to go through trivial information that wastes their time and, more importantly, doesn't fulfil what is promised. Concision is key when it comes to social media branding and holding the user's attention. Authenticity is what encapsulates these trends as a whole.

In order to reach their audience and gain their following, brands have become more authentic in their self-presentation because everything is eventually exposed online. It takes only one user to tell a thousand others that a certain brand doesn't fulfil what they advertise themselves as and that brand takes a big hit. Gone are the days where companies can advertise a false quality to a naive audience and gain a benefit. The collective user-base can easily communicate online and discuss their experience with brands unlike never before, whereas before the digital online revolution the customers were isolated from each other. People used to base their opinion on brands according to advertising, and although that is still true to some extent, users now take a second step before making a purchase or supporting a brand. They observe their user-community's opinion and user experiences and form their own opinions by extension. Before making a purchase, users google the comments that previous users have made about the product or service they are interested in.

This brings us to the importance of customer service and a personalized experience in making users feel understood so as to gain their approval. Online testimonials determine a brand's digital standing, not only on social media, but on Google itself. User reviews and feedback set the precedent for a brands' social standing with the online community, and how users that are prospective customers perceive that brand. Brands are humanizing themselves in an attempt to be more relatable. Businesses care more about their customers' satisfaction than ever before—their reputation depends on it in the digital world where users can so easily interconnect. Users pay attention to brands' stances on social issues such as environmental consciousness, gender inclusivity, and overall progressive thinking. On a much simpler level, users are also attracted to brands that follow social media trends and behave like them. Brands that post popular memes, respond to users' comments on social media, and facilitate a two-way conversation gain brownie points that no paid advertising can replace.

Influencer Branding

It is difficult for any company to be regarded as socially reliable with their user-community when it comes to the reputation of its brands. It is for this reason they hire social media influencers that have a certain cachet with their target audience. Social media influencers are pivotal players in digital marketing and social media branding. Influencers are self-branded users. In the social digital realm, they are the interface between a business and the business's target audience. Their key to success is putting a face and authentic persona to the business that they represent. They are, first and foremost, users with a large social media following. These influencers are able to dodge the stigma that commercial brands so desperately try to rid themselves of—that they are a faceless company that can't socially relate to users and just want their money. So, digital influencers have become a necessary marketing investment for commercial brands by being the medium that connects brands to users on a social and personal level. Influencers are hired by brands to sponsor a product and promote it within their social media content for their social media followers to see. It's double-funnel of second-hand branding.

Users that relate to influencers see brand endorsements in their content and are more inclined to like the brand too. It's still advertising, but it is subtler and more trustworthy. Social media influencer branding has become a huge trend, and with good reason. These influencers know digital marketing more than any commercial company does; they make something out of nothing and turn themselves from the average person to a social media celebrity, a self-made, self-branded entity. They are able to turn their popularity in social media into a cash cow for themselves. The only difference between their avarice and that of the commercial companies they work for is that they are cool in the eyes of their followers. The reason for their success that rivals the endorsements on TV and in magazines of celebrities of pop music, the movies and sports is that social media creates more of an aura of intimacy compared to TV and magazines.

Brands are social media users, and user/influencers are social media brands. Self-branded users/influencers are digital media figures and content creators with an omni-channel presence and significant follower count that they have grown organically. From Instagram models to YouTubers to bloggers, influencers brand themselves by picking a niche and creating continuously engaging content for their followers. The most vital feature of an influencer's brand is themselves. Unlike traditionally branded corporations and businesses, influencers and their brand are one and the same. The influencer content creator is the user, the product, the brand, and the face of their own business. That business is their social media app, generating revenue through sponsorships, merchandise, and ads. The rise of influencers came with the emergence of social media platforms acting as facets for sharing lifestyles, opinions, and showing oneself to other users. Social exposure and reach used to be a luxury limited to celebrities celebrated in the traditional news media, now all it takes to be an influencer is relevant content with a personal touch, consistency, getting attention online and a social media app that goes viral.

You could be a nobody one day, then famous the next. Users start to like your content, consider you a friend, and suddenly you're an influencer, impacting their lives in various ways. Influencers set the foundation for social media branding trends that businesses who have gone digital now incorporate in their marketing strategy. By being authentic and directly engaging with their audience on a regular basis, social media influencers build a bond with their followers that surpasses that of the bond of traditional businesses with their customers. Social media is, in essence, free—the content of the influencer doesn't cost them money just their time. The content of some influencers is educational, for others they are purely for entertainment and aesthetic pleasure, but the sweet spot is a combination of both. Some of the most successful influencers find a way to simultaneously educate and entertain users, but it all comes down to one thing: that the users become followers when they like the influencer, who is the actual brand. Content becomes a periphery, with the influencer at the center, getting the most attention. The novelty of self-branding is rooted in the transparency of human online connection and the influencer using a universal platform to market their personality.

Some of the most famous social media influencers today are Kim Kardashian (and really her whole family), Gary Vaynerchuk, David Dobrik, Emma Chamberlain, Kylie Jenner, Michelle Phan, Nikkie Tutorials, Neil Patel, and many others. Content is boundless—fashion, beauty, marketing, entrepreneurship, psychology, cooking, and parenting are just some of the niches that influencers focus on. After gaining a notable following, influencers start expanding beyond their original niche and create more diverse content. Users who like David Dobrik's vlogs end up just liking David himself, buying his merchandise, subscribing to his podcast channel, and purchasing branded products he endorses in his content. So, it makes sense for commercial brands to utilize influencers as marketing affiliates. Content creators market for other brands by recommending it to their followers, who are more likely to engage with the brand because it was referred to them by someone they trust and like. Corporations and growing businesses advertise their brand through social media influencers who already have an established brand and following of their own, instead of chasing users' attention or invading their platforms with display ads, which are of marginal value. They get a bigger bang for their buck with influencers than with traditional forms of advertising.

The New Wave of Digital Entrepreneurship/Online Businesses

By exploiting influencer marketing a new wave of digital entrepreneurship is emerging for entrepreneurs that do not possess the capital for an advertising campaign or operating a store, i.e. a physical retail outlet. The budding entrepreneur can create their own e-commerce website and sell their products (or services but mostly products) online. During their mid-level growth phases, these entrepreneurs reach out to influencers in order to market their products or services and increase traffic to their website. Better yet, they may be established influencers themselves who came up with a business idea or partnered with someone else who had a business idea. They can then take advantage of their already existing audience to market their product or service. The PR strategy of these strictly online businesses is a digital by word of mouth one.

Digital influencers are the new age entrepreneurs. Self-branding is an extremely effective way of building user loyalty and a sense of community. By making themselves the center of their brand, influencers can experiment with multi-dimensional content and expand their sources of revenue. An example of an ideal influencer is Kylie Jenner whose family basically coined the concept of self-branding. The Kardashian-Jenner family became famous from their reality TV show, but their success in the business world is definitely owed to the way they manage their social media accounts. They endorse their shows and businesses exclusively on social media. The influencers' content links directly to their e-commerce website thanks to Instagram's business features. No ads, no search engine marketing, just their name and Instagram. Kylie Jenner's businesses, Kylie Skin and Kylie Cosmetics, are exclusively sold online. So is Kim Kardashian West's business, KKW Beauty. It's no coincidence that the product and influencer's name are one and the same— naming their product after themselves is digital marketing 101. First, it makes the users feel like using Kylie Skin will make their skin look like Kylie's. That being said, this sets up unrealistic beauty expectations for customers who are caught up in the fabricated, idealized version that people present themselves as online. Second, by simply Googling Kylie Jenner or Kim Kardashian, Kylie Skin and KKW pop up organically as brand affiliates. The extent to which these influencers are involved in the actual production process is insignificant compared to the fact that they model it themselves on Instagram. They product test and introduce new lines by wearing the skin care or make-up themselves and by posting tutorials online. They themselves are the product. Users buy Kardashian skincare to look like a Kim Kardashian, who leads beauty trends.

It is important to note, as a conclusion to this section, that not all influencer marketing is authentic and some are downright dangerous. Some influencers endorse products that are sub-par or even harmful. FitTea, a brand that promises "flat tummies" and rapid weight loss was endorsed by several small-time and big-time influencers on social media, one of them being Kim Kardashian. FitTea was exposed as a brand that manipulates users into unhealthy eating habits for the sake of attaining unrealistic beauty standards much like the image of Kim Kardashian and other influencers with seemingly "perfect" bodies. Some influencers do indeed endorse products that are harmful, socially disruptive, or psychologically invasive. Others endorse brands they engage with themselves, and recommend beneficial products they actually use to their followers. Influencers are far from perfect and although they have a major responsibility when it comes to product promotions and how they influence the consumption habits of their audiences, there is no way to police them. The ultimate responsibility lies with the users, who are the ones that need to detect inauthentic messages. Users are beginning to develop an acute sense of brand, influencer, and product analysis that allows them to take control of influencer advertising before it takes control of them.

Use of Private Data for Targeted Advertising

It is common knowledge that for the most part folks dislike the advertising they are bombarded with. People have an innate rejection to ads, be they analogue or digital. They are regarded as manipulative and infringing. When advertising first became popular on broadcast radio and TV, magazines, newspapers and physical billboards, people would passively assume product legitimacy since marketers presented idealized versions of their products or services to the public. Over time, consumers developed a natural wariness of ads by realizing their deceitful messages that aim at mass selling sub-par products falsely portrayed as optimal. The people felt cheated and are therefore on guard with ads. The digital age and online advertising have changed that game—digital marketing has pivoted in strategy, leaning away from deception and more towards authenticity. Is this just another deceitful strategy that will be exposed? Can ads, influencer be truly authentic and honest? Or will advertising always have an underlying manipulative core? Novel advertising methods on digital platforms have us all guessing, but users are beginning to catch on to the impact that social media and search engine ads have on our user experience and consumption habits.

Ads on social media have become a more integrated part of the user experience rather than as obvious trespassers. Personalized advertising, also known as targeted advertising, allocates specific ads to a specific set of people based on their user persona and search history. In other words, if you input a search for Adidas sneakers on the websites of Adidas, Amazon, or Google, you can expect ads for the similar Adidas sneakers to appear on your Facebook and Instagram feed. These ads can seem relevant and less disruptive at first, but users are growing tired of their feeds being stuffed with marketing campaigns despite the source being a brand they regularly engage with. Targeting people with ads that are more relevant to their interests has become counterproductive. One quick search on Amazon results in an almost instant appearance of pertinent ads on the user's social media feeds. At first, users think, "At least these ads are relevant to what I'd usually like to buy, as opposed to products and services that do not apply to my lifestyle". But after being targeted with the same Amazon ads for days on end, users start to think, "If I search for a toaster on Amazon, they're going to bombard me with kitchen appliance ads via Facebook for days on end, so I'm just going to avoid the search all together".

Targeted marketing on social media and search engine displays have served online brands well in the past, creating a direct line of contact with their relevant customers based on their searches. But this process is gradually leading to a counter-revolution led by users that are tired of being overwhelmed with consumption-based ads that target them for the sake of their money. Instead of giving them a better online experience, digital advertising has driven users to a point where their self-loyalty is more important than their brand loyalty (and rightfully so). Instead of making ads a more native addition to the user experience, digital advertising methods have made ad campaigns even more intrusive and, frankly, annoying. History is repeating itself; everyday people are less susceptible to the deception of traditional advertising, and online users are facing a mirroring experience with digital advertising. People grew tired of traditional advertising's facade, and users are now rejecting digital ads in the same sense; despite being personalized, ads are still ads, and users see right through them. Users are speaking out about the shortcomings of digital advertising and creating a domino effect in which other users are coming to the same realization. There's nothing users trust more than other users.

Targeted Ads: Data is the New Oil

The general user should be aware of how their personal data affects their user experience and how it is used to manipulate the content and ads they see on their personal feed. Digital ads are highly personalized and target specific users according to their online persona, data, behavior, consumption habits, and culmination of search engine inputs. Everyone has an online user persona that overlaps with their real persona to different extents. Targeted advertising is a method used by conglomerates to direct specific ads to audiences with a specific set of character traits determined by the data that search engines and tech giants have collected about them. As mentioned previously, users are becoming more and more aware of how they are being targeted, but so long as they are browsing online and engaging with brands, they are authorizing websites to collect their personal data which is then sold to other companies. The companies that indirectly acquire the user's data can target them with ads even if the user has never searched for or directly engaged with that company before. This makes it harder for users to control their UX because it is then manipulated by factors outside of their personal searches and online habits. Despite users' active awareness and increasingly conscious online behavior, they will inevitably still be hit with targeted ads. It's an unavoidable feature of digital life.

Users are now protecting their data more, but how much of their data can they reclaim? Is our online experience rooted in free will? Or is it deterministic? There is a conspiracy theory that has been circulating on digital platforms concerning our smart devices and how they may be collecting data on users by listening in on private conversations. Research has yet to confirm or deny this claim, which has been made by a vast number of users. There's no hard evidence. Facebook claims that it "does not use your phone's microphone to inform ads or to change what you see in News Feed. Some recent articles have suggested that we must be listening to people's conversations in order to show them relevant ads. This is not true." Users claim that they talk about something random with a friend without actually searching for it, and ads appear out of nowhere the next day. According to a nationally representative phone survey of 1,006 U.S. adults conducted by Consumer Reports in May 2019, 43% of Americans who own a smartphone believe their phone is recording conversations without their permission. Could our iPhones actually be listening to us, or is this just a modern myth ignited by how effective targeted advertising is? The truth is, there's no shortage of ways in which our data can be collected, and listening in on our audio actually takes way more effort than using our browsing history and having AI efficiently take care of the rest. Still, it's peculiar to me (MR) that my boss once suggested an online fitness company, Peloton, and I got ads for it on my Instagram the next day. He even joked "Don't bother looking it up, now that we've spoken about it you'll get an ad with a 50% discount offer." I did indeed refrain from searching for Peloton or anything fitness related that day, but still got the ad. With a discount offer for new users. Despite this specific experience, and many others that users have shared, it's possible that target marketing is just *that good*.

Companies from Google on down to the small-time developers of gaming apps routinely record users' personal information—names, birthdates, credit card info —simply by asking us for it. Facebook monitors our browsing habits beyond the confines of its own platform via the often unnoticeable and disregarded image file known as a Facebook Pixel. This Pixel and other 'cookies' that are placed on websites across the Internet to track what you watch, read, and shop for benefit you with a personalized experience, but also benefit companies in ad efficiency and their promotion of hyper-consumption. Google and companies like it combine data from multiple sources, creating user profiles and personas for ad targeting purposes. The profiles created for us are built on a complex, multifaceted web of data that is, at this point, beyond our control.

Data-collecting media-monopolies are not limited to tech giants and e-companies. Governments are also a form of mega-monopolies that take advantage of user data. Politics is a profitable business, and political groups target users with manipulative advertising and propaganda to influence voting. They even make use of celebrities to influence votes (Kanye West with Donald Trump, for example). The Facebook-Cambridge Analytica data scandal exposed in 2018 revealed what a major role they played in the 2016 US election that shook the world, exposing just how much digital platforms take advantage of user information. Millions of users' personal data were harvested from their Facebook profiles, without their consent, and used for targeted political advertising. According to the Trump campaign's digital operations chief, Cambridge Analytica worked with representatives from Facebook and Alphabet Inc. (Google) on Trump's digital campaign activities. Russia was also endorsing Donald Trump and Brexit through Facebook advertising and fake news articles, targeting the right people based on their user persona and susceptibility. In the next chapter we will look at the way nation states use a form of online branding to achieve their nefarious national goals. There is an information war segmenting users and influencing voting, social opinions, and political affiliations. Targeting, be it political, social, or commercial, poses a threat to democracy in a global village as complex as the digital world. Digital advertising is shaping real-world outcomes and distorting our democracies as we traditionally understand them.

PART IV

THE SPLINTERNET, CYBER WARFARE AND THE SOCIAL MEDIA COUNTER REVOLUTION

The Splinternet and Social Media Censorship in China, North Korea, Vietnam, Russia, and the Islamic World

The Splinternet

The Internet and the World Wide Web, which host social media are not so world-wide as is suggested in the opening lines of the Wired magazine article "California Could Soon Have its own Version of the Internet":

> The Chinese Internet is not like the internet in the rest of the world. More than 150 of the world's 1,000 most popular internet sites are blocked in China, including Google, YouTube, Facebook, and Twitter. Instead, domestic platforms like Baidu, WeChat, and Sina Weibo thrive. Internet freedom advocates have worried that the internet will fracture into multiple national "splinternets" since France banned Yahoo's ecommerce users from selling Nazi paraphernalia in the country in 2000, whether due to state censorship or well-intentioned policies that alter the web experience. The Tor Project says at least a dozen countries, including Pakistan and Russia, censor the Internet. Meanwhile, search results within the European Union can differ from those else-where due to its right to be forgotten law, and Web publishers around the world are still grappling with the effect of the sweeping EU privacy regulations that took effect this year. A series of laws passed in California this year raise a new possibility: that individual US states will splinter off into their own versions of the internet (https://www.wired.com/story/california-could-soon-have-own-version-internet/ accessed Feb. 3, 2019).

Although for some the Internet was the harbinger of a united global society believing that McLuhan's notion of 'global village,' would be one of peace and harmony. In actuality the reality is quite the opposite as McLuhan (1997) himself once warned:

> The more you create village conditions, the more discontinuity and division and diversity. The global village absolutely ensures maximal disagreement on all points. It never occurred to me that uniformity and tranquility were the properties of the global village … The tribal-global village is far more divisive - full of fighting - than any nationalism ever was. Village is fission, not fusion, in depth … I don't approve of the global village. I say we live in it.

The threat of the Balkanization of the Internet or the splinternet comes from censorship through

> attempts to regulate content at national borders. These would either turn the Internet into a patchwork of unpredictably unreliable access to information or a lowest-common-denominator medium hosting only the most universally acceptable (i.e., blandest) content … [Although] various countries do filter and censor, the Internet's somewhat porous quality has largely survived, even though some people can't access some types of information at some times from some locations
>
> (https://blogs.lse.ac.uk/medialse/2013/11/18/unified-field-the-splinternet/ #comments, accessed March 27, 2020).

Evgeny Morozov writing in Foreign policy shares this concern:

> Google, Twitter, Facebook— are U.S. companies that other governments increasingly fear as political agents. Chinese, Cuban, Iranian, and even Turkish politicians are already talking up "information sovereignty" a euphemism for replacing services provided by Western Internet companies with their own more limited but somewhat easier to control products, further splintering the World Wide Web into numerous national Internets. The age of the Splinternet beckons (https://foreignpolicy.com/ 2010/04/26/think-again-the-internet/ accessed January 5, 2019).

A second concern re the Balkanization of the Internet is about

> addressing an issue of technical Internet governance overseen since 1998 by the International Corporation for Assigned Names and Numbers. Although there are many registrars selling domain names and many registries (one for each country and generic top-level domain), ultimately transforming human-friendly domain names into the numbers that computers use is a monopoly distributed by 13 root servers. The feasibility and dangers of splitting the root have been the subject of many debates and disputes over the years. Snowden has revived the uneasiness outside the US about ICANN's remaining ties to the US Department of Commerce. The upshot is much

more interest in other, more international governance efforts such as the Internet Governance Forum … Still, what scares people about this is not so much Balkanization as that the participation of so many governments with conflicting regulatory agendas could stall the Internet's development entirely (https://zine.openrightsgroup.org/ features/2013/unified-field-the-splinternet accessed January 5, 2019).

Internet Censorship

With the exception of most democratic states almost all other countries have some form of Internet censorship that varies with the political climate of the country at various times. The mechanism for Internet censorship on a national level is not difficult to achieve as networks are highly centralized in most countries with data being sent through a central routing system. "These nodes essentially serve as choke points where a single switch can turn the Internet off; governments and ISPs [Internet Service Providers] usually control these switches" (https://www. cloudwards.net/internet-censorship/ accessed Feb.19, 2019).

There is a work-around for Internet censorship by private users through VPN (virtual private network) mechanisms that allows them to access the Internet without the restrictions imposed by their governments. A VPN "enables users to send and receive data across shared or public networks as if their computing devices were directly connected to the private network. Applications running across a VPN may therefore benefit from the functionality, security, and management of the private network (https://en.wikipedia.org/wiki/Virtual_private_ network accessed Feb. 19, 2019)."

The Chinese Internet Scene: The Great Chinese Firewall and the Golden Shield

The policy of the Chinese government to control and monitor the use of the Internet domestically has given rise to the creation of the Great Chinese Firewall whereby only Internet content sanctioned by the government is allowed to penetrate China. In addition to not allowing popular Web sites from entering the country the Chinese government closely monitors all Internet posts through the development of a software that enables the government to monitor and or intercept any online information that is sent or received. It also has the ability to block domain names and destination IP addresses. An army of 2 million or more officials with the title of "internet public opinion analyst" are employed by government, private corporations and news services to keep a watchful eye on all posts on the Chinese Internet and to delete those that violate government guidelines. Many of the censors are hired by Chinese companies to make sure that they do not run afoul of government regulations as the Chinese government demands that they censor themselves and police their content.

The fact that it is known that an army of government agents are monitoring the Internet, private Chinese citizens for the most part self-censor themselves and conform to the following regulations in place since 1997 shortly after the Internet was allowed into China:

> No unit or individual may use the Internet to create, replicate, retrieve, or transmit the following kinds of information:

1. Inciting to resist or breaking the Constitution or laws or the implementation of administrative regulations;
2. Inciting to overthrow the government or the socialist system;
3. Inciting division of the country, harming national unification;
4. Inciting hatred or discrimination among nationalities or harming the unity of the nationalities;
5. Making falsehoods or distorting the truth, spreading rumors, destroying the order of society;
6. Promoting feudal superstitions, sexually suggestive material, gambling, violence;
7. Terrorism inciting others to criminal activity; openly insulting other people or distorting the truth to slander people;
8. Injuring the reputation of state organizations;
9. Other activities against the Constitution, laws or administrative regulation (https://en.wikipedia.org/wiki/Internet_censorship_in_China accessed January 5, 2019).

In addition to weeding out unwanted posts the government throughs its propaganda agencies and through its encouragement of government employees numbering in the hundreds of thousands post millions of propaganda messages online. They are known as the "50 Cent Party" in reference to the 50 cents they are presumably paid for each post.

Despite these regulations a group of researchers, Qin, Stromberg, and Wu (2017) that carried out a study of Chinese social media including 13.2 billion blog posts found,

> that a shockingly large number of posts on highly sensitive topics were published and circulated on social media ... [They found] millions of posts discussing protests and an even larger number of posts with explicit corruption allegations. [The researchers concluded that although] this content may spur and organize protests, it also has the benefit to the regime of making "social media effective tools for surveillance. [They

found that] most protests can be predicted one day before their occurrence and that corruption charges of specific individuals can be predicted one year in advance.

The major Chinese social media sites include the following:

Douban.com is a Chinese social networking service website allowing registered users to record information and create content related to film, books, music, recent events and activities in Chinese cities. It has 47 million registered users.

Qzone is a social media website that was created by Tencent, a Chinese multinational investment conglomerate consisting of Internet related services, entertainment, AI and technology holdings. Qzone allows users to write blogs, keep diaries, send photos, listen to music, and watch videos. It has 480 million registered users.

The **Renren Network** is a social media app, popular among college students that is similar to Facebook. Renren in Chinese literally means everyone's network. It has 160 million registered users.

Sina Weibo is a micro-blogging website, the Chinese version of Twitter. It has 300 million registered users.

The North Korean Internet Scene: Uriminzokkiri

The North Korean regime has an even more restrictive censorship of the Internet than China with only a very few top government officials with access to the global Internet. For those with a need to communicate with fellow North Koreans in order to carry out their government, scientific, or commercial duties there is the Uriminzokkiri, which is basically an internal intranet with no connection to the outside online world. Uriminzokkiri can be accessed outside North Korea at http://www.uriminzokkiri.com. It also posts to

- Facebook (https://www.facebook.com/Uriminzokkiri-124452740935216/),
- Twitter (https://twitter.com/uriminzok?lang=en) and
- Flickr (https://www.flickr.com/photos/uriminzok/) for propaganda purposes, but North Koreans are not allowed to access these three services.

The term Uriminzokkiri is a Korean portmanteau of 'among or between us minjok', where minjok is a term that represents the Korean people, ethnicity or nation with a hint of racism as the child of a Korean and a non-Korean would not be considered minjok. Uriminzokkiri operated the intranet that certain privileged North Koreans are permitted to access. They provide news provided by the government-controlled news service Korean Central News Agency (KCNA), which is the only news service in the country. KCNA provides news stories for both internal and external consumption. It controls and operates all the newspaper, radio and television services in the country.

The Vietnam Internet Scene

Like other communist regimes the Vietnamese government does not allow any anti-communist or anti-government content. It has arrested and jailed a number of bloggers who have defied its regulations regarding what can be appropriately discussed.

The Russian Internet Scene

Russian use of the Internet developed more slowly than was the case in the West but by the end of 2015 it represented 70% of the population. Internet censorship in Russia exists but it is not at the same level as that in China or North Korea. What began as an attempt to ban sites advocating or promoting drug use, describing methods of suicide, child pornography was then expanded to include extremist material, basically code for anti-regime political material and certain religious sites. The list of such material, the Federal List of Extremist Materials, contained 3,762 items by August of 2016. The production, storage or distribution of these materials is considered a criminal offense in Russia.

In addition to these restrictions the government also monitors Internet usage. The government requires companies that provide Internet services to record the user data of all its customers and store that information on a server that the government can access. In addition, all cafes, restaurants and hotels that operate publicly accessible Wi-Fi hotspots must record and store the information of all the users of their hotspot.

The major Russian social media sites include:

- LiveJournal, a blogging site used by Russian speakers both within Russia and in diaspora. It has 17.6 million registered users.
- Odnoklassniki, a social media site connecting former schoolmates that is popular in Russia and former Soviet republics. It has 45 million registered users.
- VK.com, a social media site, including music upload, listening and search that is popular in Russia and former Soviet republics. It has 250 million registered users.

The Islamic Countries Internet Scene

Most Islamic countries have some form of censorship, some due to consideration of morality and some for political reasons. Authorities in Iran have blocked access to the following social media sites: Instagram, Facebook, YouTube and Telegram claiming they are a threat to national security. The most popular social media sites in Iran are: Facenama, the Iranian version of Facebook, Aparat.com, an Iranian YouTube-like site and Twitter.

The Saudi Arabian regime blocks content that is regarded as "immoral" under Islamic laws as well as content that attacks the royal family or any of its policies especially any content connected with terrorist organizations.

The Pakistani regime has rather strict restrictions mostly focused on political matters, but some restrictions related to religious and cultural concerns also exist. In Egypt the regime of President Abdel Fattah al-Sis has greatly restricted the use of the Internet and the press as well specifically targeting terrorism and what it calls extremism. Turkish authorities exercise tight control of the Internet primarily for political reasons. The situation in the Gulf states, Syria, and Iraq is similar to that of Pakistan, Egypt and Turkey.

Internet censorship in Indonesia, Malaya and Bangladesh are not as severe as is the case in other Islamic states and is focused primarily on morality issues such as their ban on pornography.

References

McLuhan, Marshall. 1997. "The Hot and Cool Interview, with Gerald Emanuel Stearn." In *Media Research. Technology, Art, Communication*, edited by Michael A. Moos, 45–78. Amsterdam: Routledge.

Qin, Bei, David Stromberg, and Yanhui Wu. 2017. "Why Does China Allow Freer Social Media? Protests versus Surveillance and Propaganda," *Journal of Economic Perspective* 31 (1): 117–140.

CHAPTER TWENTY-ONE

World War III: Cyber Warfare and Social Media Threats to Democracy

World War III is a guerrilla information war with no division between military and civilian participation—Marshall McLuhan (1970, 66)

Introduction

Marshall McLuhan was predicting the key role information would play in world geopolitics long before the commercial release of the Internet in 1994 and even before Arpanet, the forerunner of the Internet was a going reality. The above quote was published in 1970 and written sometime in 1969 the same year Arpanet transmitted it first message. McLuhan made his prediction of cyberwarfare before he was even aware of the Arpanet and decades before the emergence of the Internet and the World Wide Web. Two years later McLuhan and Nevitt (1972, 152) wrote about a connection between technological development and war:

It is easy to view war in terms of technological development:

WORLD WAR I - A RAILWAY WAR OF CENTRALIZATION AND ENCIRCLEMENT.

WORLD WAR II - A RADIO WAR OF DECENTRALIZATION CONCLUDED BY THE BOMB.

WORLD WAR III - A TV GUERRILLA WAR WITH NO DIVISIONS BETWEEN CIVIL AND MILITARY FRONTS (upper case used in the original source).

McLuhan's prediction of World War III as an information-based war is connected to what he saw was the effects of electrically configured information. He wrote, "War is never anything less than accelerated technological change ... Now that man has extended his central nervous system by electric technology, the field of battle has shifted to mental image making and breaking, both in war and in business (McLuhan 1964, 102)."

McLuhan based his prediction on the fact that a hot war was no longer viable because, with nuclear weapons, no one could win a such a war which in all likelihood would result in the total annihilation of both antagonists and probably the rest of humanity. He wrote: "The nuclear bomb will turn warfare into the juggling of images (McLuhan 2011, 360)."

Another aspect of his prediction of World War III as an information war was his notion of the global village and his observation that, "the unformulated message of an assembly of news items from every quarter of the globe is that the world today is one city. All war is civil war. All suffering is our own (McLuhan 1995, 291)." It is also worth mentioning that contrary to the popular notion that the global village would be a place of harmony, that McLuhan actually thought the exact opposite:

> The closer you get together, the more you like each other? There's no evidence of that in any situation that we've ever heard of. When people get close together, they get more and more savage, impatient with each together ... The global village is a place of very arduous interfaces and very abrasive situations (From the television interview on The Education of Mike McManus show, TV Ontario, December 28, 1977)

Murtaza Hussain (2017) credits McLuhan with predicting the emergence of cyberwarfare:

> Decades before smartphones the internet, and social media, philosopher Marshall McLuhan, who worked on media theory, predicted a future world war fought using information ... McLuhan's prediction may have felt outlandish in his own era, but it seems very close to our present-day reality. Decades ago, the barriers to entry for broadcasting and publishing were so high that only established institutions could meaningfully engage in news dissemination. But over the past 10 to 15 years, ordinary individuals have been radically empowered with the ability to record, publish, and broadcast information to millions around the world, at minimal cost ... For better or worse, thanks to social media and smartphones, a version of the "guerilla world war" predicted by Marshall McLuhan – a war over information drawing in states,

militaries, activists, and ordinary people in equal measure – has come into existence. The consequences are likely to transform politics, conflict, and daily life for generations to come. McLuhan himself suggested that surviving in this new world would be possible only through a conscious embrace of change, rather than a retreat into reactionary policies.

We are in the midst of a cyberspace world war that pits the democratic or largely democratic states against three communist or formerly communist regimes, namely Russia, China and North Korea as well as the radical Islamic movements consisting of ISIL (The Islamic State of Iraq and the Levant) and also known as ISIS (The Islamic State of Iraq and al-Sham or The Islamic State of Iraq and Syria); Boko Haram; Al-Shabaab, Al-Qaeda, the Taliban; and the Caucasus Emirate. To a certain degree one can include Iran in this group as they fund certain terrorist groups that are allied with them politically and militarily.

Cyberwar involves a number of fronts some of which involve social media which will be the focus of this chapter. We will focus on the use of social media to disrupt democracy by influencing the way people vote and by exacerbating internal divisions between different social groups in the targeted nation. Another form of cyber warfare of which we will be concerned is the use of social media that is deployed to recruit individuals to join terrorist organizations abroad or to radicalize individuals and encourage them to engage in terrorists acts locally. Cyber warfare also involves both military and commercial espionage as well as the hacking of cyber infrastructure. While cyberwar activities do not primarily involve the use of social media they are still of interest so as to understand the full scope of cyberwarfare and the different fronts on which this form of war is conducted. We therefore review in this chapter the use of social media to conduct cyber warfare in general.

Russian Cyber Attacks Using Social Media

The Russians engage in cyber warfare on a number of fronts that include:

1. influencing elections so that candidates in other countries are elected or referendums are decided that are in the national interest of Russia and
2. to sow internal strife so as to weaken the states that they target with a special focus on Ukraine, the EU and the USA.

The most notorious examples of the latter were their interference in the 2016 American presidential election that resulted in Donald Trump's victory and their interference in the United Kingdom's Brexit referendum. In the case of Trump's election, they secured an inhabitant of the Oval Office who was friendly to their interests. In the Brexit case by helping to secure a yes vote through a campaign of misinformation they actually achieved their goal of the UK's withdrawal from and the weakening of the European Union as well as the British economy. These two cases are not the only examples of Russian interference in democratic elections. The Russians also attempted to interfere in the elections in Ukraine, France, Germany, Austria, the Netherlands, the Czech Republic, Norway and Bulgaria (https://www.washingtonpost.com/news/monkey-cage/wp/2018/01/05/russia-has-been-meddling-in-foreign-elections-for-decades-has-it-made-a-difference/?utm_term=.955d30179fa3, March 19, 2019).

Russia's Internet Research Agency

The Internet Research Agency (IRA) known in Russia as Агентство интернет-исследований (Agentstvo Internet Issledovaniy) is a Russian company, based in Saint Petersburg that engages in online activities to influence events in other countries for the benefit of their clients in government and business. They are reported to have close ties to Vladimir Putin and the Russian Intelligence Agency. They are basically a troll farm where a troll is an agent who provokes dissents and/or starts quarrels in online communities such as a forum or a social media site. The troll's objective is to illicit an emotional response and thereby to incite discord or provoke the recipient to take some action that will benefit the troll or the troll's client. In the case of the Russian IRA they have gained notoriety in a number of arenas, namely the political and social affairs of the Ukraine, the United States, Great Britain and the countries of the Middle East. In addition to international trolling IRA also does domestic trolling in which it praises Vladimir Putin and Bashar al-Assad, supports all of the governments positions and criticizes the Russian opposition. Their modus operandi is to create fake accounts on social media sites, discussion boards, online video sites such as YouTube and those of newspapers, both online and in print. The IRA also used its fake accounts on social media sites to organize protests of various kinds, many that were racially charged. They organized or promoted protest rallies in Buffalo; Baltimore; Stone Mountain, Georgia; Houston; Lawrence, Kansas; Orlando; St. Paul, Minnesota; Dallas; Chicago; Twin Falls, Idaho; Washington DC, Charlotte. North Carolina; and New York City. (https://en.wikipedia.org/wiki/Internet_Research_Agency, accessed March 19, 2019).

Evidence of Russian Interference in the American Presidential Election

As early as 2015 the FBI warns the Democratic National Committee (DNC) that their computers had been compromised and are transmitting information back to Russia. In March 2016 John Podesta, Hillary Clinton's campaign manager fell victim to a phishing expedition and all of his emails were captured and subsequently released by hackers and WikiLeaks. In October of 2016 just, days before the presidential election the Department of Homeland Security and the Office of the Director of National Intelligence on Election Security released a report indicating that the Russians were behind the "compromises of e-mails from US persons and institutions, including from US political organizations (https://www.usatoday.com/story/news/politics/onpolitics/2016/10/21/17-intelligence-agencies-russia-behind-hacking/92514592/, accessed March 19, 2019.)."

In December 2016 just after the presidential election, the Washington Post reported that "the CIA has concluded in a secret assessment that Russia intervened in the 2016 election to help Donald Trump win the presidency (https://www.washingtonpost.com/world/national-security/obama-orders-review-of-russian-hacking-during-presidential-campaign/2016/12/09/31d6b300-be2a-11e6-94ac-3d324840106c_story.html?utm_term=.a9aaa397c89f, accessed January 2, 2019)."

Days before leaving office President Obama orders sanctions against the Russians for their part in the presidential campaign hacking. In July of 2017 a bipartisan bill preventing Trump from easing sanctions on the Russians passed the Senate 98 to 2 and the House of Representatives 419 to 3.

Facebook revealed in September of 2017 that over 3,000 advertisements posted on its site between June 2015 and May 2017 were linked to Russia. An article in the Washington Post reported that the ads were placed by Russia's Internet Research Agency (IRA). The ads that were posted were placed in battle ground states to have the maximum effect on the outcome of the election to boost Trumps chances over those of Hillary Clinton. Facebook was not the only social media site that the Russians used.

Internet Research Agency, also organized a campaign entitled "Don't Shoot Us" aimed at black voters in which they posed as Black Lives Matter on Facebook, Instagram, Pokémon Go, Tumblr, Twitter and YouTube. The campaign highlighted police brutality towards blacks inciting them to protest as well as fomenting divisiveness in American society. The donotshoot.us Web site was registered to a nonexistent person, Clerk York, who gave an address and phone number that belongs to a shopping mall in North Riverside, Illinois (https://money.cnn.com/2017/10/12/media/dont-shoot-us-russia-pokemon-go/index.html).

Robert Mueller indicted 12 members of the Russian Intelligence Agency, GRU, accusing them of hacking emails and computer networks associated with the Democratic party during the 2016 presidential campaign.

Russian meddling in the election did not happen through hacking election counting machines but rather by the creation of fake accounts in social media sites as we have just described. The Russians infiltrated numerous social media sites. They then created

> messages aimed at the most divisive issues in American culture. For relatively little expense, Russian operatives got into Facebook, opened numerous fake accounts, set up external websites to corroborate, and then unleashed messages and allowed followers and fans to like, share, post, and repost. People unwittingly distributed messages cooked-up to play upon issues of strife and dissention. Russians used algorithmic data to predict which people were most vulnerable to certain kinds of messages. This helped further polarize U.S. culture, especially by means of anti-Hillary information, right up to the election. Along these same lines, I'm not sure how many people here know that the 'California secession site' had been hosted in Russia (Anton 2018).

Russian interference continued in the USA 2018 and again in 2020 election and will probably be an ongoing fact of life.

Chinese Espionage and Cyber Attacks

The Chinese unlike the Russians for the most part focus their cyber-attacks on commercial and military espionage with the exception Taiwan where it has attempted to influence the outcomes of elections there (www.bloomberg.com/news/articles/2018-09-19/chinese-cyber-spies-target-taiwan-s-leader-before-elections, accessed March 21, 2019). Therefore, social media does not play a prominent role in their cyber-attack strategy. We will summarize their external cyber-attack activities nevertheless for the sake of completeness and then turn to their cyber security activities internally that very much involve social media. Chinese cyberwarfare is considered a bigger threat to the countries it targets than the Russians, North Koreans and the Iranians according to Crowdstrike (https://www.telegraph.co.uk/technology/2018/10/09/china-ahead-russia-biggest-state-sponsor-cyber-attacks-west/, accessed March 21, 2019).

The Chinese target any country, government agency, NGO, company, university or research institute where they can gather information to further their commercial activities or strengthen their military position, which is the main focus of their cyber-attacks. It is hard to determine the source of Chinese cyber-attacks but there is evidence that they are carried out by both government agencies and Chinese companies. The targets of Chinese cyberwarfare include government agencies with complaints from the USA, Canada and India. Companies that have been attacked include Google, Northrup Grumman, Symantec, Yahoo, Dow Chemical, Adobe Systems, Siemens, Moody's Analytics, Trimble, Apple and Amazon as well as other technology companies in the "pharmaceutical, defence, mining and transport sectors (https://en.wikipedia.org/wiki/Chinese_espionage_in_the_United_States, accessed March 19, 2019)."

Chinese Cyber-Security and the Social Credit System

The Chinese authorities conduct a form of cyber warfare against its own citizens through its internal cyber-security activities and its social credit system. The Chinese social credit system is a nation-wide surveillance of its citizens operated by the government through monitoring their postings on social media and all other Internet-based communications and their behavior in public through a network of security cameras, which number 200 million circa 2018 but is expected to triple in number in the very short term. Each citizen in China is evaluated by social credit system by which they gain or lose points. Any criticism of the government results in the loss of points and any form of criminal activity but so does any of the following behaviors: jay walking, buying too much alcohol, not paying bills or taxes on time. Having a low social credit score can result in being barred from air and train travel, having one's social media accounts shut down, one's Internet connection slowed down, having one's children excluded from special schools, and being shut out of various elite occupations. Also, many employers will be reluctant to hire a person with a low social credit score.

North Korean Cyber-Attacks

North Korea has achieved a very sophisticated and high level of expertise in conducting cyber warfare which some experts consider to be in the league of that of the Russians and the Chinese. They have successfully broken into computers causing mischief and actually stolen currencies. Its cyber warfare arsenal is regarded as a bigger threat than its nuclear and missile arsenal as a nuclear attack would lead to its annihilation but its cyber-attacks have proven to be devastating and there is not a remedy to stop them (https://www.scmp.com/week-asia/geopolitics/article/2187363/north-korean-cyberwarfare-big-threat-its-nuclear-weapons).

Kim Jong-un has been reported to say by the Washington-based think tank, the Centre for Strategic and International Studies, that, "Cyber warfare, along with nuclear weapons and missiles, is an 'all-purpose sword' that guarantees our military's capability to strike relentlessly" (https://www.scmp.com/week-asia/geopolitics/article/2187363/north-korean-cyberwarfare-big-threat-its-nuclear-weapons, accessed September 19, 2019).

"It's been reported the regime has long been sending its best students to study computer science and cybersecurity in China's top universities ... Estimates put North Korea's cyber army at about 6,000 hackers, and their cyber capabilities are both a weapon and also a source of income for the country (ibid.)."

A major source of hard currency for North Korea has been its stealing of crypto currencies. "The numerous attacks on small and private companies have led to allegations that Pyongyang is hacking into cryptocurrency exchanges to steal virtual money, like Bitcoin, said Seungjoo Kim. Stolen cryptocurrencies are attractive because they are difficult to trace back to their original owner (https://www.voanews.com/east-asia-pacific/where-did-north-koreas-cyber-army-come, accessed September 19, 2019)."

One of the favourite targets of North Korean hackers is South Korea. They have broken into "South Korean computers to steal confidential information about next-generation fighter aircraft and other weapons" as well as gathering "the names, addresses and birth dates of almost 1,000 defectors living in South Korea from a refugee resettlement centre—potentially endangering their families and friends still living in the hermit kingdom

(https://www.scmp.com/week-asia/geopolitics/article/2187363/north-korean-cyberwarfare-big-threat-its-nuclear-weapons, accessed September 19, 20019)."

Hacktivism

There is some validity to McLuhan's claim "that all war is civil war in the Information Age. Hacktivism (a portmanteau of hacking and activism) is in a certain sense a form of civil war. Hacktivists for the most part attack targets in the country in which they reside so one could say they are engaged in civil war as the purpose of their hacktivism is not to conquer another country but to promote a cause such as social change or a political objective to which they are dedicated. While hacktivists claim that their actions are a form of civil disobedience carried out in cyberspace, their activities are considered, in almost all jurisdictions, as illegal.

References

Anton, Corey. 2018. "Comments on "How to Fix Facebook,"MEA Convention 2018. Presentation at the 2018 Media Ecology Convention in Orono Maine. Private Communication in an Email Entitled "MEA Follow-Up" that Corey Anton Sent to Bob Logan on July 11, 2018.

Hussain, Murtaza. 2017. "The New Information Warfare." *The Intercept (November 25, 2017)* (https://theintercept.com/2017/11/25/information-warfare-social-media-book-review-gaza/, accessed Jan 1, 2019).

McLuhan, Marshall. 1964. *Understanding Media: Extensions of Man.* New York: McGraw Hill. (The page references in the text are for the McGraw Hill paperback second edition. Readers should be aware that the pagination in other editions is different.)

McLuhan, Marshall. 1970. *Culture is Our Business.* New York: McGraw-Hill.

McLuhan, Marshall. 1995. "I. About Media." In *Essential McLuhan,* edited by Eric McLuhan and Frank Zingrone. Concord Ontario: Anansi.

McLuhan, Marshall. 2011. Book of Probes. Berkeley, CA: Gingko Press

McLuhan, Marshall, and Barrington Nevitt. 1972. *Take Today: The Executive as Dropout.* Toronto: Longman Canada.

CHAPTER TWENTY-TWO

The Social Media Counter Revolution

Introduction

Many of the very people who created the social media digital revolution are in revolt opposing the very environment they helped to create. The counter revolutionaries are for the most part not the gazillionaire owners of the social media companies that they founded, but rather they are the engineers, programmers, and designers that created the addicting features of social media and in some cases were early investors and champions of these social media apps. In this chapter we will for the most part bring you the very words of these social/digital media rebels who have spoken out against the very problems they helped to create. We quote them in full because paraphrasing them would not have the same impact as sharing their eloquent critiques. We have also quoted extensively from journalists who have written about these rebels for much the same reason. We conclude the chapter and hence the book with a discussion of whether or not social media should be regulated and, if so, to what extent.

The Facebook Counter Revolutionaries

Justin Rosenstein who created the 'like' feature of Facebook that has become the ubiquitous feature of so many other social media apps is critical of his own 'like' feature. In his defense for creating 'likes' Rosenstein said: "It is very common for humans to develop things with the best of intentions and for them to have unintended, negative consequences (P. Lewis 2017)."

Justin Rosenstein has taken steps to limit his own exposure to social media. He has tweaked his laptop's operating system to block Reddit, banned himself from Snapchat, which he compares to heroin, and imposed limits on his use of Facebook. But even that wasn't enough. In August, the 34-year-old tech executive took a more radical step to restrict his use of social media and other addictive technologies. Rosenstein purchased a new iPhone and instructed his assistant to set up a parental-control feature to prevent him from downloading any apps.

> He was particularly aware of the allure of Facebook "likes", which he describes as "bright dings of pseudo-pleasure" that can be as hollow as they are seductive. And Rosenstein should know: he was the Facebook engineer who created the "like" button in the first place.

> A decade after he stayed up all night coding a prototype of what was then called an "awesome" button, Rosenstein belongs to a small but growing band of Silicon Valley heretics who complain about the rise of the so-called "attention economy": an internet shaped around the demands of an advertising economy (ibid,).

Other examples of criticism from within the social media community include the following:

"Over the weekend, some highly placed, anonymous Facebook employees told the *New York Times* that they've been questioning the company's role in the campaign. Five more anonymous employees told *BuzzFeed* on Monday that they and dozens of others within Facebook have formed a secret 'task force' to advocate for stronger action against fake news (Oremus 2016)." "Several current and former Facebook employees tell NPR there is a lot of internal turmoil about how the platform does and doesn't censor content that users find offensive (Shahani 2016)." Folks at Facebook both present and past are critical of their company as the following excerpt from an article on the Facebook crisis indicates:

> But the monomaniacal focus on social platforms' influence on the election had the effect of drawing out some of Facebook's earliest champions and builders. They criticized what they themselves had built. The first was Justin Rosenstein, now the co-founder at Asana, a collaboration software company. Rosenstein helped to lead development on Facebook's like button, but this year he complained about the psychological effects of social media, and the "bright dings of pseudo-pleasure" that came from friends liking his posts … Roger McNamee, an early Facebook investor, said the company is directly responsible for the misuse of its platform by Russians. "Facebook did not set out to increase political polarization and empower bad actors to undermine democracy, but this outcome was inevitable," he wrote in an October op-ed in USA Today. "It was the

result of countless Facebook decisions, all made in pursuit of greater profits. In order to maximize its share of human attention, Facebook employed techniques designed to create an addiction to its platform (Newton 2017)."

Another critic by an insider is Sean Parker, the first president of Facebook and a billionaire, who now heads the Parker Institute for Cancer Immunotherapy. He admitted that Facebook knowingly created an app that would be addictive and that would exploit what he called "a vulnerability in human psychology (https://www.theguardian.com/technology/2017/nov/09/facebook-sean-parker-vulnerability-brain-psychology)." At an event in 2017 Parker described himself as

> something of a conscientious objector ... I don't know if I really understood the consequences of what I was saying, because [of] the unintended consequences of a network when it grows to a billion or 2 billion people and ... it literally changes your relationship with society, with each other ... It probably interferes with pro-ductivity in weird ways. God only knows what it's doing to our children's brains (Newton 2017).

Chamath Palihapitiya, a venture capitalist and an early executive at Facebook has also been critical of his former employer with whom he made a fortune. "Palihapitiya spoke at Stanford's business school last month and had harsh words for his former employer, saying 'Facebook and other social networks are de-stroying how society works.' He also implied that early Facebook employees didn't do enough to stem 'unforeseen consequences' of abuse on the platform (Kovach 2017)."

Palihapitiya is turning his critique of Silicon Valley into action through the venture capital company, Social Capital, that he founded. Its mission statement is as follows: "Our mission is to advance humanity by solving the world's hardest problems. We believe that empowering entrepreneurs who seek to improve the lives of the people around them is the best way to create more opportunity glob-ally (www.socialcapital.com)." Palihapitiya is obviously doing penance for his early days at Facebook much like Sean Parker who is concerned with finding a cure for cancer.

Tristan Harris, the Center for Humane Technology and the "Time Well Spent" Movement

Tristan Harris, a design ethicist at Google for three years, was concerned with the impact of the Silicon Valley companies across the globe. He expressed the fol-lowing sentiments:

A handful of people, working at a handful of technology companies, through their choices will steer what a billion people are thinking today ... I don't know a more urgent problem than this. It's changing our democracy, and it's changing our ability to have the conversations and relationships that we want with each other (P. Lewis 2017).

Harris acting on his conviction quit Google and founded the Center for Humane Technology and inspired the associated "Time Well Spent" movement. He revealed the way that social media trap their users to stay with them to the advantage of the social media company and to the disadvantage of the users in a paper entitled, "How Technology is Hijacking Your Mind—from a Magician and Google Design Ethicist":

Where does technology exploit our minds' weaknesses? I learned to think this way when I was a magician. Magicians start by looking for *blind spots, edges, vulnerabilities and limits* of people's perception, so they can influence what people do without them even realizing it. Once you know how to push people's buttons, you can play them like a piano. And this is exactly what product designers do to your mind. They play your psychological vulnerabilities (consciously and unconsciously) against you in the race to grab your attention. I want to show you how they do it.

Hijack #1: If You Control the Menu, You Control the Choices ...

Hijack #2: Put a Slot Machine in a Billion Pockets. If you're an app, how do you keep people hooked? Turn yourself into a slot machine. One major reason why is the #1 psychological ingredient in slot machines: intermittent variable rewards ...

Hijack #3: Fear of Missing Something Important (FOMSI). Another way apps and websites hijack people's minds is by inducing a "1% chance you could be missing something important" ...

Hijack #4: Social Approval. We're all vulnerable to **social approval.** The need to belong, to be approved or appreciated by our peers is among the highest human motivations. But now our social approval is in the hands of tech companies ...

Hijack #5: Social Reciprocity (Tit-for-tat). We are *vulnerable to needing to reciprocate others' gestures.* But as with Social Approval, tech companies now manipulate how often we experience it ...

Hijack #6: Bottomless bowls, Infinite Feeds, and Autoplay. Another way to hijack people is to keep them consuming things, even when they aren't hungry anymore. How? Easy. *Take an experience that was bounded and finite, and turn it into a bottomless flow that keeps going* ...

Hijack #7: Instant Interruption vs. "Respectful" Delivery. Companies know that messages *that interrupt people immediately are more persuasive at getting people to respond* than messages delivered asynchronously (like email or any deferred inbox). In other words, **interruption is good for business …**

Hijack #8: Bundling Your Reasons with Their Reasons. Another way apps hijack you is by taking *your reasons* for visiting the app (to perform a task) and *make them inseparable from the app's business reasons* (maximizing how much we consume once we're there) …

Hijack #9: Inconvenient Choices. We're told that it's enough for businesses to "make choices available." Businesses naturally *want to make the choices they want you to make easier, and the choices they don't want you to make harder*. Magicians do the same thing. You make it easier for a spectator to pick the thing you want them to pick, and harder to pick the thing you don't …

Hijack #10: Forecasting Errors, "Foot in the Door" strategies. Lastly, apps can exploit people's inability to forecast the consequences of a click. People don't intuitively forecast the *true cost of a click* when it's presented to them. Sales people use "foot in the door" techniques by asking for a small innocuous request to begin with ("just one click to see which tweet got retweeted") and escalate from there ("why don't you stay awhile?"). Virtually all engagement websites use this trick (https://medium. com/thrive-global/how-technology-hijacks-peoples-minds-from-a-magician-and-google-s-design-ethicist-56d62ef5edf3).

Associated with the Center for Humane Technology is the "Time Well Spent" movement which defines the problem they are addressing in the following terms:

> Our society is being hijacked by technology. What began as a race to monetize our attention is now eroding the pillars of our society: mental health, democracy, social relationships, and our children. What we feel as addiction is part of something much bigger. **There's an invisible problem that's affecting all of society.**

Facebook, Twitter, Instagram, and Google have produced amazing products that have benefited the world enormously. But these companies are also caught in a **zero-sum race for our finite attention,** which they need to make money. Constantly forced to outperform their competitors, they must use increasingly persuasive techniques to keep us glued. They point AI-driven news feeds, content, and notifications at our minds, continually learning how to hook us more deeply—from our own behavior.

Unfortunately, what's best for capturing our attention isn't best for our well-being:

- Snapchat **turns conversations into streaks,** redefining how our children measure friendship.
- Instagram **glorifies the picture-perfect life,** eroding our self-worth.
- Facebook **segregates us into echo chambers,** fragmenting our communities.
- YouTube **autoplays the next video within seconds,** even if it eats into our sleep.

These are not neutral products. They are part of a system **designed to addict us.** The race for attention is eroding the pillars of our society.

The whole system is vulnerable to manipulation. Phones, apps, and the web are so indispensable to our daily lives—a testament to the benefits they give us—that we've become a captive audience. With two billion people plugged into these devices, technology companies have inadvertently enabled a direct channel to manipulate entire societies with unprecedented precision.

Technology platforms make it easier than ever for bad actors to cause havoc:

- Pushing lies directly to specific zip codes, races, or religions.
- Finding people who are already prone to conspiracies or racism, and automatically reaching similar users with "Lookalike" targeting.
- Delivering messages timed to prey on us when we are most emotionally vulnerable (e.g., Facebook found depressed teens buy more makeup).
- Creating millions of fake accounts and bots impersonating real people with real-sounding names and photos, fooling millions with the false impression of consensus.

Meanwhile, the platform companies profit from growth in users and activity (http:// humanetech.com/problem/ accessed Dec 17, 2018).

The Maggerman Counter Revolution

Another counter revolutionary is David Maggerman, a computer scientist who became a multi-millionaire working at Renaissance Technologies that was owned by David Mercer. Mercer also owned Cambridge Analytica, the firm that used Facebook data to influence the American 2016 election and the United Kingdom's Brexit campaign. It was the election of Donald Trump that caused Maggerman to break with Mercer and realize that what he was doing was unethical. He described his epiphany about his work at Renaissance Technologies by describing the company in the following terms as "a place that uses really bright people, who could do a lot of great things in the world — and simply has them sit at their desks and make money from money." He saw the Internet as a dystopic technology saying, "we are creating social and emotional and psychological cancer for society through how technology is infiltrating and being adopted." He decided to work to create a better Internet. To that end he joined other angel investors at Differential Ventures with the objective of supporting new start-ups that will help transform the Internet into a better place that supports human values rather than a place where people's personal data is exploited for unethical purposes. Maggerman also donated $400,000 to the Freedom from Facebook Movement.

The Freedom from Facebook Movement describes its objectives on its Web page, https://freedomfromfb.com (accessed January 19, 2019) as follows:

Facebook has too much power over our lives and democracy. It's time for us to take back that power.

Most of us use Facebook, Instagram, WhatsApp, and Messenger. They're important ways for us to communicate and connect with each other.

But Facebook and Mark Zuckerberg have amassed a scary amount of power. Facebook **unilaterally decides the news** that billions of people around the world see every day. It buys up or **bankrupts potential competitors** to protect its monopoly, killing innovation and choice. It **tracks us almost everywhere we go** on the web and, through our smartphones, even where we go in the real world. It uses this intimate data hoard to **figure out how to addict us** and our children to its services. And then Facebook **serves up everything about us** to its true customers -- virtually anyone willing to pay for the ability to convince us to buy, do, or believe something.

And it is **spending millions on corporate lobbyists**, academics, and think tanks to ensure **no one gets in their way.** Enough!

The five members of the Federal Trade Commission, which is the part of our government tasked with overseeing Facebook, can make Facebook safe for our democracy by breaking it up, giving us the freedom to communicate across networks, and protecting our privacy.

Together, we will make sure that they do.

The Freedom from Facebook movement according to a report in Wired magazine (https://www.wired.com/story/freedom-from-facebook-open-markets-institute/ , accessed January 20, 2019) has engaged in an active campaign against Facebook including the following actions:

In July 2018 they sat behind Monika Bickert as she testified to the US Congress with signs 'depicting Sheryl Sandberg and Mark Zuckerberg's heads atop an octopus whose tentacles reached around the planet.' During Facebook's shareholder meeting they chartered an airplane 'to fly overhead with a banner that read YOU BROKE DEMOCRACY.' They "filed a complaint with the Federal Trade Commission asking the agency to investigate a Facebook breach ... that affected 30 million user accounts (ibid.)."

Facebook recognizing that The Freedom from Facebook was a real threat hired Definers Public Affairs, a right leaning opposition research group, to fight Freedom from Facebook as well as George Soros. Facebook cut their ties to Definers following an article in the NY Times revealing their connection to Definers (en. wikipedia.org/wiki/Definers_Public_Affairs, accessed January 20, 2019).

Brichter, Jobs, and Lanier

Loren Brichter, who created the pull-to-refresh mechanism, which he considers to be addictive has come to the realization that smartphone addiction has reduced the quality of his life. In response to this realization he "has blocked certain websites, turned off push notifications, restricted his use of the Telegram app to message only with his wife and two close friends, and tried to wean himself off Twitter … He charges his phone in the kitchen, plugging it in at 7 pm and not touching it until the next morning (P. Lewis 2017)."

Steve Jobs, the driving force behind the iPod, iPad and the iPhone, when asked what his children thought of the iPad responded by saying, "They haven't used it. We limit how much technology our kids use at home (ibid.)."

Jaron Lanier (2018) is a pioneer of the digital media revolution particularly with respect to virtual reality. He has come out strongly against social media with his book *Ten Arguments for Deleting Your Social Media Accounts Right Now* with the following arguments:

1. You are losing your free will;
2. Quitting social media is the most finely targeted way to resist the insanity of our times;
3. Social media is making you into an a**hole;
4. Social media is undermining truth;
5. Social media is making what you say meaningless;
6. Social media is destroying your capacity for empathy;
7. Social media is making you unhappy;
8. Social media doesn't want you to have economic dignity;
9. Social media is making politics impossible;
10. Social media hates your soul.

Fighting Smartphone and Social Media Addiction

Some users of smartphones and social media have joined the counter revolution. Here are the poetic confessions of two smartphone addicts who kicked the habit after coming to the realization how precious time is in the real world.

Dear iPhone—It Was Just Physical, and Now It's Over

I can't count the number of times I pulled out my phone just for the feeling of unlocking the screen and swiping through applications, whether out of comfort—like a baby sucking her thumb—or boredom—like a teenager at school, tapping his fingers on a desk. In those cases, I sought not mental stimulation, but physical release.

[Some] may see a smartphone extending my mind, but I could feel it dulling my senses. Without my phone, I'm more fully myself, both in mind and body. And now, more than ever, I know that looking at my phone is nothing compared to looking at my daughter while the room sways as I rock her to sleep, or how shades of indigo and orange pour in through the window and cast a dusky glow over her room, or the way her warm, milky breath escapes in tiny exhalations from her lips, or how the crickets outside sing their breathless, spring lullaby. See, once I looked up from my phone, I remembered that each experience could be a symphony for the senses, just like it had been when I was a child and, thank God, there was no such thing as smartphones (Katie Reid on http://nautil.us//blog/dear-iphoneit-was-just-physical-and-now-its-over accessed on May 1, 2018).

Here is Lydia Sohn's description of how she was able to manage her smartphone addiction:

Basic Smartphone Guidelines That Have Made My Life More Fulfilling

#1: Play with My Kid: On the afternoons I am with my son, I put my phone in my purse.

#2: Be Present to Family and Friends: I keep my phone away when I am with my husband, parents, siblings and friends.

#3: Be Bored from Time to Time: I try to let myself be bored from time to time.

#4: Have Fun on Vacations: I severely limit my smartphone use during vacations.

#5: Don't Use the Smartphone as a Social Crutch: My smartphone also goes away for any kind of work meeting or social gathering.

#6: Give My Smartphone an Early Bedtime in a Different Room: my phone has been going to "bed" in the kitchen at 9 p.m. while I go into my own bedroom to read, journal and talk to my husband (https://medium.com/@lydia.sohn/basic-smartphone-guidelines-to-strengthen-my-relationships-99a359c22af accessed October 24, 2018).

The User Counter Revolutionaries: The High-Tech Refuseniks

While there are many social media counter revolutionaries among the creators of social media and their users as we have documented, there is another class of counter-revolutionaries worthy of our attention, namely the high-tech refuseniks. Social media thrives on the use of the latest hardware devices. Keeping up with the latest version of the iPhone or Android device is part and parcel of those that use and thrive on social media. There is another counter revolutionary movement forming namely the high-tech refuseniks as documented in an article entitled The Hi-Tech Refuseniks (https://www.independent.co.uk/life-style/gadgets-and-tech/features/the-hi-tech-refuseniks-1787793.html, accessed December 27, 2018). In the article Nick Harding reports that, "Phones and TVs are 'obsolete' the moment they hit the shops, to tempt us with newer models. But now consumers are fighting back …"

Today's high-tech digital devices de rigueur for social media are quickly out of date because of the rapid rate at which the manufacturers update their equipment with new features. Upgrading is often a costly and, in most cases, unnecessary because the so-called out-dated equipment is perfectly functional. There are those who have an almost religious devotion to the latest version of their equipment, particularly among Apple aficionados. But many are now realizing that constantly upgrading their equipment is a losing proposition and they are getting off "the upgrade treadmill (https://lifehacker.com/5942915/how-to-get-off-the-upgrade-treadmill-and-stop-wasting-money-on-new-tech, accessed December 29, 2018)."

Conclusion: The Good, Bad and Ugly of Social Media

As we have mentioned throughout this study, and as observed by McLuhan, all media and all technologies create both service and disservice. In Chapter Six—The Impacts of Social Media we described some of the services (good) and the disservices (bad) of social media. In Chapters Seventeen and Eighteen we touched on the disservice (bad) of digital media monopolies such as Facebook, Instagram, Google and Amazon. In this chapter we have described the disservices (bad) of social media identified by some of the actual creators of social media.

In light of the events that took place on January 6, 2021, namely the insurrection of the Trump supporters that attacked, entered and desecrated the U.S. Capitol in their attempt to overthrow the government and reverse the outcome of the 2020 presidential election we must mention some of the truly ugly and evil disservice aspects of social media. Although the insurrectionists were directly egged on by Trump's rhetoric in an outdoor rally held in the morning of January 6th, the MAGA (Make America Great Again), movement that he created and mobilized was a direct result of his use of social media. Twitter served as the medium for his assault on the truth, the tens of thousands of out-right lies and the biggest lie of all that he actually won the 2020 election, that the election was rigged and that it was stolen from him despite the fact that the Republicans actually increased their numbers in the House of Representatives. As pointed out by Timothy Snyder (2017) in his book *On Tyranny: Twenty Lessons from the 20th Century*, "lies can lead to fascism." Trump and his followers misuse of Twitter is the ugly side of the disservice of social media. And it was not only Twitter but other forms of social media that allowed these enemies of democracy to organize themselves into a movement that has shook the very roots of the democracy of the American republic.

Hitler made use of radio and the loudspeaker to create his racist Nazi movement. These technologies were relatively new in the 1930s when Hitler undermined Germany's democratic government. Social media such as Facebook, Instagram and Twitter are also relatively new technologies that emerged in the past 25 years. It is interesting that Twitter finally realized the harm it created when it finally banned Trump from using Twitter as a way to prevent him from doing any further damage after the January 6 fiasco.

To Regulate or Not to Regulate

The story of the January 6th episode, which is not yet over as we write these words, is a cautionary tale. Given the damage that has been wrought serious thought must be given to how social media needs to be regulated. If today's democracies have agencies to regulate public broadcaster such as the The Canadian Radio-television and Telecommunications Commission here in Canada, the Federal Communications Commission in the USA and the European Commission in the European Union serious thought must be given to a commission (perhaps an international one) to regulate the operation of social media companies such as Facebook, Instagram and Twitter. Freedom of speech does not allow one to cry fire in a crowded theatre to cause a stampede.

Freedom of speech does not allow one to cry fire in a crowded theatre to cause a stampede. Freedom of speech should not allow social media to allow its users to post anti-democratic, fascist, racist, or other dangerous forms of fake news and incitements to encourage illegal acts. It is easy for us to condemn the posting of such material but the challenge will be how to exactly define what kind of material should be banned. Just as the legal system has a judicial system to judge what acts are illegal, a judicial system should be created to determine what material needs to be regulated on social media. We would argue that a social media platform that allows messages to be posted that act as incitements to encourage illegal acts would be libel under existing conspiracy laws. It is beyond our expertise to suggest how this social media regulatory system should be organized but it is clear to us in light of our analysis of social media there is a need for such a system. And the events of

January 6, 2020 in Washington DC and the presidency of Donald J. Trump make it clear that serious thought needs to be given to this issue and a mechanism to protect democracies from the abuses of social media must be developed.

References

Kovach, Steve. 2017. "Facebook Responds to Former Exec Who Feels 'Tremendous Guilt' for What He Helped Make," accessed January 13, 2018 on https://www.businessinsider.com/facebook-responds-chamath-palihapitiya-criticism-social-media-201-12.

Lanier, Jaron. 2018. *Ten Arguments for Deleting Your Social Media Accounts Right*. New York: Henry Holt and Co.

Lewis, Paul. 2017. "'Our Minds Can Be Hijacked': The Tech Insiders Who Fear a Smartphone Dystopia." Manchester Guardian, October 6, 2017.

Newton, Casey. 2017. "In 2017, Key Facebook Builders Disowned Their Creations." https://www.theverge.com/2017/12/20/16800842/facebook-2017-russia-scandal-news-feed-criticism-defectors, accessed February 16, 2018.

Oremus, Will. 2016. "The Real Problem Behind the Fake News" http://www.slate.com/articles/technology/technology/2016/11/the_problem_with_facebook_runs_much_deeper_than_fake_news.html, accessed October 2, 2018.

Shahani, Aarti. 2016. "From Hate Speech to Fake News." https://www.npr.org/sections/alltechconsidered/2016/11/17/495827410/from-hate-speech-to-fake-news-the-content-crisis-facing-mark-zuckerberg, accessed August 21, 2018.

Snyder, Timothy. 2017. *On Tyranny: Twenty Lessons from the 20th Century*. New York: Tim Duggan Books a subsidiary of Penguin Random House.

Appendix—Social Media Apps

From (https://en.wikipedia.org/wiki/List_of_social_networking_websites#cite_note-89).

The table published in the book was accessed January 15, 2021. To update the table below the reader might wish to hit the link above to get the most up to date list.

Name	Focus	Date launched	Registra-tion Require-ments, if any	Global Alexa Inter-net page ranking as of May 25, 2020
8tracks.com	Streaming user-curated playlists	8 August 2008	None	17,106
23snaps	Parents save photos, videos, measurements and stories of their children	June 2012	None	734,955
About.me	Promote individuals	October 2009	None	8,898
Academia.edu	Academics/researchers	September 2008	None	270
alimero	Blog	2011	None	49,060
Amikumu	Language learners	22 April 2017	None	3,856,270
aNobii	Books	2006	None	50,569
Anphabe.com	Employment website	2011	None	119,534
aSmallWorld	European jet set and social elite worldwide	March 2004	Invitation system	211,403
Athlinks	Running, swimming	2001	None	105,354
Band	Group communication, South Korea		None	3,174,387
beBee	Personal brands	February 8, 2015	None	16,004
BeWelcome	Homestays and hospitality	2007	None	372,044
BigMuscle.com	Physically fit gym guys	21 February 1999	None	616,245
Biip.no	Norwegian community	1 June 2005	Requires Norwegian phone #	8,796,911
BlackPlanet	Black Americans	1 September 1999	None	45,531
Busuu	Language learning community	16 May 2008	None	9,057
Buzznet	Music and pop-culture	2005	None	57,573

Care2	Green movement	1998	None	64,031
CaringBridge	Connections after a serious health event.	1997	Age 18+,[20]	25,757
CarSwap	Car swap and sales matching platform.	2016	None	3,091,224
Cellufun	Mobile Social-network game	2007	Age 14+	1,808,258
Chess.com	Chess players	May 2007	None	414
Chictopia	Fashion enthusiasts	2008	None	166,892
Classmates.com	Alumni	1995	Age 18+	17,16
Cloob	Popular in Iran	2004	None	9,103
CouchSurfing	Homestays and hospitality	June 12, 2004	Age 18+; $15/year fee	11,071
CozyCot	East Asian and Southeast Asian women	2001	None	1,328,076
Crunchyroll	Anime fans	2006	None	459
Cucumbertown	Chefs	2012	None	1,779,064
Cyworld	Popular in South Korea.	1999	None	45,153
DailyStrength	Medical & emotional support community	November 4, 2007	None	476,880
Dayviews	Sweden	2007	None	106,609
DeviantArt	Art community	August 7, 2000	Age 13+	424
Diaspora*	Distributed social network	November 2010	None	NA
Discord	live chat and voice for groups	2015	Age 13+	
douban	Chinese movies, books, and music	2005	None	301
Doximity	U.S. medical doctors	March 2011	U.S. physicians only	31,680
Draugiem.lv	Popular in Latvia, Lithuania, Hungary)	April 24, 2004	Invitation only	16,662

Continued

Name	Focus	Date launched	Registra-tion Require-ments, if any	Global Alexa Inter-net page ranking as of May 25, 2020
Dreamwidth	Blogging	2009	None	18,580
DXY.cn	Chinese health care professionals	July 23, 2000[41]	None	2,761
Elixio	Business executives jet set and global elite	July 2007	Invitation system	4,343,472
Ello	Creative field	March 2014[43][44]	Invitation system	47,128
English, baby!	Students and teachers of English as a second language	2000	None	157,793
eToro	Social investing, finance	May 2007	None	877
Experience Project	Life experiences	2007	None	201,357
Experts Exchange	IT professionals	1996	None	11,360
Facebook	Photos, videos, blogs, apps	February 2004	Age 13+	4
Faces	Women in digital media	1997	None	N/A
Fandalism	Musicians	January 2012	None	884,496
Fetlife	BDSM	January 2008	"Legal age to see adult content"	3,104
FictionCity	Artists	2011	None	N/A
Fieldoo	Soccer players	February 25, 2013	None	1,492,734
FilmAffinity	Movies and TV series	2002	None	2,696
Filmow	Movies and TV series	2009	None	10,052
Fishbrain	Fishing	2010	None	195,428
Fitocracy	Fitness	February 2011	None	250,318

Flickchart	Movie ranking	September 9, 2009	None	240,160
Flickr	Photo sharing, commenting, photography related networking	February 2004	Age 13+	758
Flixster	Movies	January 20, 2006	Age 13+	68,083
Focus.com	Business-to-business	2005	Age 13+	220,728
Fotki	Photo and video sharing	October 1998	None	42,35
Foursquare	Location-based mobile social network	2009	None	4,486
Friendica	Distributed social network	July 2010	None	1,553,830
Fyuse	Photography, 3D images	2014	None	1,159,809
Gab.com	Right-wing politics	2016	None	10,423
Gaia Online	Anime and games	2003	Age 13+	34,339
Gapyear.com	Travel	July 1998	None	37,602
Gays.com	LGBT	16 May 2008	None	3,297,201
Gaysir	Gays and bisexuals in Norway	September 22, 2000	None	1,052,862
Geni.com	Families, genealogy	January 16, 2007	None	8,816
Gentlemint	Men	November 25, 2011	None	519,340
GetGlue	Entertainment	October 28, 2008	None	203,003
Goodreads	Library cataloging, book lovers	December 2006	None	313
GovLoop	Government employees	May 2008	None	150,431
Grindr	Gay and bisexual men	March 2009	None	57,642

Continued

Name	Focus	Date launched	Registra-tion Require-ments, if any	Global Alexa Inter-net page ranking as of May 25, 2020
Habbo	Teenagers	August 2000	Age 13+	42,886
hi5	Video games	2003	Age 13+	4,870
Hospitality Club	Homestays	2000	None	611,620
HR.com	Human resources professionals	1999	None	58,575
Hub Culture	Ven digital currency	November 2002	Invitation system	1,090,409
I Had Cancer	Cancer survivors	July 2011	None	941,560
Ibibo	Talent promotion	2007	None	842,377
Identi.ca	Hackers and software freedom advocates	2008	None	162,488]
İnci Sözlük	Turkey	2010	None	42,243
Indaba Music	Musicians, remix contests, and networking	2007	None	933,756
Influenster	Product sampling and reviews	2010	None	13,740
Inspire	Healthcare professionals	January 2005	None	81,341
Instagram	Photo and video sharing	October 2010	Age 13+	30
IRC–Galleria	Finland	2000	Age 12+; Finnish language	146,274
italki	Language learning	2007	None	4,492
JamiiForums	Tanzania	2011	None	9,923
Kaixin001	Mainland China users	2008	None	12,918
KakaoStory	Pages, South Korea	March 22, 2012	None	508
Kiwibox	Teenagers	1999	Age 13+	830,833

Name	Description	Date	Requirement	Number
KizlarSoruyor	Question-based	2011	None	967
Kroogi	Artists	2007	None	148,026
Labroots	Science and medicine	2008	None	23,770
Last.fm	Music	2002	None	1,748
Letterboxd	Film	October 2011	None	2,898
LibraryThing	Book lovers	August 29, 2005	Age 13+	23,102
Likee	Videos	July 2017	None	46,809
LinkedIn	Business and professional networking	May 2003	Age 14+	62
Listography	List-sharing	2006	None	67,568]
LiveJournal	Blogging	April 15, 1999	OpenID	453
Mastodon	Micro-blogging	October 5, 2016	None	121,439
Mealshare.org	Meal coordinating service	2006	None	5,000,000
MEETin	Social meetings	2003	None	1,514,604
Meetup (website)	Offline meetings	2002	Age 18+	1,410
MeWe	Likes and emojis	2012	None	5,309
Micro.blog	Microblogging	April 24, 2017	None	94,868
Minds	Distributed social network with Ethereum tokens	June 2015[116]	None	13,342
mixi	Japan	October 25, 2000	None	4,072
MocoSpace	Mobile community	2005	Age 14+	67,463
MocoSpace	Mobile social network	2005	None	67,757
MouthShut.com	India	2003	None	7,333

Continued

Name	Focus	Date launched	Registra-tion Require-ments, if any	Global Alexa Inter-net page ranking as of May 25, 2020
Mubi	Auteur cinema	2007	None	8,425
MyHeritage	Family	2003	None	7,834
Myspace	General	August 2003	Age 13+	2,417
Nearby	People nearby	June 2010	None	306,158
Nexopia	Canada	2003	Age 13+[126]	511,049
Ning	Create social networks	2005 (Networks 2007)	Age 13+	3,779
NK.pl	School, college and friends in Poland	2006	None	20,638
Odnoklassniki	Connect with former classmates in Russia	March 4, 2006	None	64,566
Open Diary	Blog	1998	Age 13+	448,282
Parler	Free speech and privacy	2018	None	84,729
Partyflock	Electronic dance music	10 November 2001	Age 18+	183,622
PatientsLikeMe	Patients with life-changing illnesses	2006	Age 13+	138,581
Peach	Mobile	January 2016	None	2,203,922
PEERtrainer	Weight loss	October 2005	None	169,439
Pink Petro	Women working in the petroleum industry	2014	None	1,188,288
Pinterest	Pinboard for organizing and sharing things you love	2011	None	149
Pixnet	Taiwan	2003	None	103
Plaxo	Aggregator	2002	None	196,912

Play.fm	Disc jockeys	2004	None	108,273
Playlist.com	Music	2006	Age 13+	156,931
Plurk	Micro-blogging, RSS in Taiwan	2008	None	1,176
Portfolium	Student employment search	2014	None	92,370
Postcrossing	Send and receive postcards	14 July 2005	None	63,264
Quora	Questions and answers	2009	None	243
Qzone	In Simplified Chinese; caters for mainland China users	1995	None	NA
RallyPoint	Military veterans	2014	None	58,028
Ravelry	Knitting and crochet	2007	None	7,594
Readgeek	Book recommendations	December 2010	None	770,688
Reddit	News aggregator, social bookmarking, and Internet forums	June 23, 2005[149]	None	19
Renren	China	December 2005	None	1,217
ReverbNation.com	Musicians and bands	2006	Age 16+	8,713
Rooster Teeth	Social network and community site	October 4, 2004	Age 13+	12,596
Ryze	Business	2001	Closed	315,852
Sarahah	Feedback from friends and coworkers	November 2016	None	26,675
Sharesome	Pornography	10 January 2018	Age 18+[156]	76,644
Sina Weibo	Microblogging in mainland China	August 14, 2009	None	16
Skoob	Brazilian readers	2009	None	5,094
Skyrock	French-speaking world	2002	None	7,098
Snow	Image messaging	September 2015	None	748,795

Continued

Name	Focus	Date launched	Registra-tion Require-ments, if any	Global Alexa Inter-net page ranking as of May 25, 2020
Sonico.com	Latin America and Spanish and Portuguese speaking regions	2007	Age 13+	205,504
SoundCloud	Repository of original music pieces	2007	None	104
Soup.io	Microblogging	April 2007	None	13,039
Spaces	Russian mobile phone users	2006	None	180,920
Spot.IM	A service for webmasters to add social net-working functionality to their websites	2012	None	20,886
Stage 32	Professionals in film, television and theater	February 2012	None	62,265
Steam	game launcher, forums, live chat/	2003	None	
StudiVZ	University students, mostly in German-speaking countries.	2005	None	321,295
Tagged	Tagging similar photos and profiles	October 2004	None	1,764[169]
Talenthouse	Creative collaboration	June 2009	None	55,658
Taringa!	Argentina	2004	Age 13+	1,345
TermWiki	Learning / languages / translation	May 2010	None	121,336
The Sphere	Luxury network with exclusive personalized services	December 2008	Invitation system	6,324,962
Thinkspot	Free speech alternative to Patreon	2019	None	168,140
Total Recut	Video sharing and resources website for fans and creators of video remixes	2017	None	1,655,943
Travellerspoint	Travel	2002	None	80,909

Tuenti	Phone company in Spain with social networking service	2006	None	154,087
Tumblr	Micro-blogging	February 2007	None	119
Twitter	Micro-blogging, RSS, updates	July 15, 2006	None[179]	48
Twoo.com	Disc jockeys	2011	None	2,239
Untappd	Beer drining	October 2010	None	19,687
Vampirefreaks.com	Gothic and industrial subculture	1999	Age 13+	397,773
Viadeo	Business owners, entrepreneurs and managers	2004	None	18,339
Vingle	Photos	October 21, 2011	None	20,718
Virb	Artists, including musicians and photographers	2007	None	276,328
VK	Music upload, listening and search. Popular in Russia and former Soviet republics.	September 2006	None	23
Voat	Censor free reddit clone	2014	None	
Warm Showers	Homestays and hospitality while bicycle touring	2005	None	474,297
Wattpad	Readers and authors	2006	None	488
WAYN	Travel and lifestyle	May 2003	Age 18+	100,569
We Heart It	Image sharing	2008	None	2,528[191]
Werkenntwen	General	2006	None	180,637
Wooxie	Blogging and micro-blogging	2009	None	1,707,357

Continued

Name	Focus	Date launched	Registra-tion Require-ments, if any	Global Alexa Inter-net page ranking as of May 25, 2020
WriteAPrisoner.com	Inmates connect with friends, family	September 2000	Age 18+	108,122
WT Social	Subwikis	October 2019	None	128,961
Wykop.pl	Micro-blogging	December 25, 2005	None	3,230
Xanga	Blogs and "metro" areas	1998	None	126,187
XING	Business primarily in Germany, Austria, and Switzerland	2003	None	1,877
Yammer	Office colleagues	2008	Must have company email	2,184
Yelp	Business review	2004	None	550
Yo	Quick connections	April 1, 2014	None	765,260
zoo.gr	Greeks	2004	None	76,968

UNDERSTANDING MEDIA ECOLOGY

Lance Strate
General Editor

This series is devoted to scholarship relating to media ecology, a field of inquiry defined as the study of media as environments. Within this field, the term "medium" can be defined broadly to refer to any human technology or technique, code or symbol system, invention or innovation, system or environment. Media ecology scholarship typically focuses on how technology, media, and symbolic form relate to communication, consciousness, and culture, past, present and future. This series is looking to publish research that furthers the formal development of media ecology as a field; that brings a media ecology approach to bear on specific topics of interest, including research and theoretical or philosophical investigations concerning the nature and effects of media or a specific medium; that includes studies of new and emerging technologies and the contemporary media environment as well as historical studies of media, technology, and modes and codes of communication; scholarship regarding technique and the technological society; scholarship on specific types of media and culture (e.g., oral and literate cultures, image, etc.), or of specific aspects of culture such as religion, politics, education, journalism, etc.; critical analyses of art and popular culture; and studies of how physical and symbolic environments function as media.

For additional information about this series or for the submission of manuscripts, please contact:
Lance Strate, Series Editor | *strate@fordham.edu*

To order other books in this series, please contact our Customer Service Department:
peterlang@presswarehouse.com (within the U.S.)
orders@peterlang.com (outside the U.S.)

Or browse online by series:
www.peterlang.com

www.ingramcontent.com/pod-product-compliance
Lightning Source LLC
Chambersburg PA
CBHW050645280326
41932CB00015B/2788